Endorsements

"As a father of three children and a grandfather of 11 children, I learned early on that every child is different! I also learned that parents have to raise their children according to their child's way. What I love about *Unicorn Parenting* is the affirmation that we also raise our children according to our unique way. Author Julie Giles writes, 'This book is not about how to parent but how you parent and why.' With a fun online survey, she breaks down parenting into 18 different styles with a corresponding animal that best exemplifies your parenting style. Then she gives help on how to be better at your style. The best parents are those who really know their kids and really know themselves. *Unicorn Parenting* will help you do both."

—Jim Tomberlin Pastor, Author,
Church Consultant with The Unstuck Group

"*Unicorn Parenting* is one of the best parenting books I've come across in years. Julie offers a fresh and creative approach to being a better parent, but she also will help you discover your own unique parenting style. I highly recommend this wonderful resource."

—Jim Wideman Children & Family Ministry Pioneer
Nashville, Tennessee
www.jimwideman.com

"Even though my kids are still young, I found this parenting assessment to be so valuable. The insights into which parenting styles are most intrinsic to who I am were both helpful and thought provoking as I'm still discovering the ways I'm wired and how it will affect my home. I especially found it interesting the things you can look for in a parenting partner, and I look forward to my husband taking the assessment and the discussions that will come from this as we learn how to parent our kids better together. I'm thankful for the space to grow as a mom and the insights this book has helped me gain."

—Bethany Straarup
Associate Pastor Elevation Church

"I hate glitter... And I'm not a huge fan of unicorns. But there is value in facing those uncomfortable facts, which is what *Unicorn Parenting* is designed to do. In classic Julie Giles style, she walks alongside us, encouraging us to dig a little deeper, push back the reservations, and dive into knowing ourselves better— not just for the sake of self-actualization, but for the benefit of our greatest occupation: rearing our children. There's a lot to dig into here - and layers to uncover. The parenting assessment is both complex and simplified. It has real meat in a digestible format that makes it fun and informative. Don't be fooled by its adorable analogies. There is significance if you really sit with the idea that you are unique. Being intentional about those unique strengths and weaknesses is where your power and influence as a parent take on a new level. Julie reminds us of the foundational facts of what is good parenting while celebrating the differences we each bring to the table. As a parent, you are unique. *Unicorn Parenting* is a unique parenting book, unlike any other, and deserves to hold a spot among the best resources an intentional parent can have."

—Denise Marti Lion mama of three,
Founding Director of Providence: A Christian Montessori Community
Author of the Pesto Parent Blog, and Lifelong Learner

"Julie Giles has given us a fresh, unique, and powerful approach to parenting. Developed for the 21st century and rooted in Scripture. I loved the Parenting STYLES! To raise children who will love God and become the persons who He made them to be, read *Unicorn Parenting*."

—David E. Clarke, Ph.D.
Christian psychologist, podcaster, YouTuber, and author of fifteen books

Unicorn Parenting

A STYLE as unique as YOU!

Julie Giles

Copyright © 2022 by Julie Giles
First Paperback Edition

All rights reserved. No part of this publication may be reproduced, distributed, or transmitted in any form or by any means, including photocopying, recording, or other electronic or mechanical methods, without the prior written permission of the publisher, except in the case of brief quotations embodied in critical reviews and certain other noncommercial uses permitted by copyright law. For permission requests, write to the publisher, addressed "Attention: Permissions Coordinator," at the address below.

All Scripture quotations are taken from THE MESSAGE. Copyright © 1993, 2002, 2018 by Eugene H. Peterson. Used by permission of NavPress. All rights reserved. Represented by Tyndale House Publishers, Inc.

Published by Freiling Publishing,
a division of Freiling Agency, LLC.

P.O. Box 1264
Warrenton, VA 20188

www.FreilingPublishing.com

PB ISBN: 978-1-956267-68-6
eBook ISBN: 978-1-956267-69-3

Printed in the United States of America

Dedication

To You –

This book is for every parent whose strategy is forming as we speak, it's worth it – all of it! Be intentional!

It is dedicated to all who have influenced my life. My parenting is a collection of your inspiration.

Thank you to my amazing husband Isaac – the perfect partner in my imperfect parenting journey.

To my kids: Heather, Jessica, Josh, Jonathan, Nikki, Penny, Crista, Justin, and Sarah, whether natural or adopted, this journey has been worth every minute! And thanks to my own parents, Stan & Jan, and my own siblings – Liz and Steve.

To Denise, Debbie, and Sarah, thank you for encouraging me to write.

—Julie
An Ant Parent whose journey
has been filled with Jesus and
a significant support system

FREE Parenting STYLE Assessment

You're invited to visit growthmindedparents.com to complete a free Parenting STYLE Assessment created as a companion to this book.

> *Your child may be influenced by a million things. Your parenting helps your kids know which matter most.*
>
> —J. Giles

Contents

Introduction xiii

Section 1
Parenting Like a Unicorn

1	Happily Ever After	3
2	The Parenting Void	9
3	The Desire to Parent Like a Unicorn	13
4	Understanding Your Strategic Parenting STYLE	19
5	Parenting Imperfectly	29
6	Parenting Perspective	39
7	Parenting with a Growth Mindset	51
8	Directionally Challenged Parenting	61
9	Culturally Independent Parenting	67
10	Parenting with a Support System	71
11	Understanding Your Unique Parenting STYLE	77
12	Your Parental Job Description	83
13	Parenting Effects	89
14	Parenting Balance	97
15	Structurally Sound Parenting	103
16	Phases of Parenting Power	115
17	Parenting Leaders	121
18	Introspective Parenting	125

Section 2
Discovering Your Parenting STYLES

The Ant Parent 131
The Bear Parent 135
The Clownfish Parent 141
The Dolphin Parent 147
The Eagle Parent 153
The Flamingo Parent 159
The Hawk Parent 165
The Lion Parent 171
The Lizard Parent 177
The Octopus Parent 183
The Ostrich Parent 189
The Otter Parent 195
The Owl Parent 201
The Penguin Parent 207
The Possum Parent 213
The Raccoon Parent 219
The Turtle Parent 225
The Whale Parent 231

Introduction

AS A PARENT, you are as unique as a unicorn! Your gifts and strengths are different from any other parent. Understanding these strengths and challenges will help you to become the best parent possible for your children.

As you read *Unicorn Parenting*, you will have many opportunities to assess your parenting decisions, your parenting reactions, and any influences that cause you to parent the way you do. An assessment has been created to help you consider how you got here. It will illuminate how the past influences your here and now. Together, we will explore how it shapes your tomorrow. We will discuss why the collective experiences of your life flow from you into your child. And we will chat about your bad habits and consider if it is possible to avoid passing them on to your children.

As you read, we will discuss the behaviors you have as an adult and how you have been shaped because of them. In the midst of your parenting issues, you have developed a parenting type or style, a set of habits that help you navigate each day.

Along with a team of parenting specialists, I have worked to develop a set of eighteen of the most common parenting types. I can't wait for you to discover which animal in nature you most closely identify with. It should be fun, enlightening, and introspective, all at the same time. We are confident that you are surrounded by many other parents whose animal types are different from your own, and exploring with your friends will make it that much more fun.

Historically, four styles have been used by psychologists to define parenting. Though they are helpful, there are many other aspects we will explore. Parenting looks a lot different in the twenty-first century, and this assessment will help you see the ways you are similar to others. It will help you decipher what it looks like to dive deeper into the discussion of your parenting, and it will help you identify why you react the way you do in life's biggest challenges.

The best part of the Parenting STYLE Assessment is that you will see who God has made you to be and where you struggle for control. Once you begin to let God be in control of your parenting habits, you will have the ability to see His blessings in your life, in your home, and in your relationship with your child.

The future holds far more possibilities than the past—in fact, the past has no possibilities at all, because we cannot change what has already happened. Far too often, we let our minds wander into the past, forgetting to look forward. When it comes to parenting, there is new promise with every new day. Tomorrow has potential ready to be discovered.

Section 1

Parenting Like a Unicorn

*I'm not raising my kids to survive the world.
I'm raising them to change it!*

—*Steven Furtick*

1

Happily Ever After

YOU HAVE OPENED this book because you are a parent, and that looks different on your side of the table than on mine. We both know there is no "how to get it right" parenting guide, and that means you need to be keenly aware of the differences. Today we are going to talk about what makes your family wonderful and about your decisions in the parenting journey. And of course, let's talk about what is going great in your home. We will chat about how to improve upon the things that are holding you back, even if it has just begun.

Before we start, let's acknowledge that parenting is not a competition, and it is not something you will get 100 percent right. In fact, you will get a lot of it wrong. But you still have to wake up each day and try to make it better. Parenting can be confusing, and the pressure to succeed can be crippling. In these pages, you will find a conversation with a friend, someone who has raised four kids and has mentored countless more. One thing I like to ask people is: "How in the world did you get here, and are you ever going to feel that you are doing a good job?"

The answer to the second half is yes, and along the journey of the first half, you will discover that in the initial eighteen years of your child's life, you will have many stories to tell. Some will be funny, some will be shocking, and others will be heartbreaking. That's part of the beauty of this significant role you are fulfilling. There will be many hard decisions to make and many moments of introspection in which you will ask even more questions. Before you know it, your child will move from this stage into the next, and some of the questions you are asking will change. Though your convictions, goals, and processes will look different from mine, your parenting mission is to fight for what matters most. This will inspire you to keep moving toward the goal of raising your child to become the most wonderful adult he or she can possibly be.

Tiny humans enter the world every day. The collective amount of time and money spent painting nurseries, selecting names, and shopping for strollers, car seats, diapers, and the avalanche of other baby paraphernalia will quite possibly be the most exhausting yet strategic experience you have ever encountered. You must not mess this up; a tiny life depends on you. The world around you would have you believe that getting this just right will provide you with parenting bliss and a wonderful life ahead. This "happily ever after" scenario could overwhelm even the most highly equipped parents and could lead you to believe that all of this stuff will help you produce the perfect child.

Providing the ideal setting for a child to be raised is important. As you have learned, child-rearing is much more about having the correct response in the moment than it is filling your online shopping cart with pink and blue ruffles while eating pickles and ice cream at 2 A.M.

The end game of parenting is presenting the world with well-rounded, well-prepared individuals who can thrive and adapt to the changes they are presented with. There's no way to know what they will face or understand how their culture will be different from what it is today. That means that preparing them for adaptability and equipping them with the ability to apply concepts to new situations is crucial. That five-star-rated car seat seems like a drop in the bucket compared to the real-time investment you have made by the time your child turns eighteen. But it's not over even at that point. Parenting is a lifelong series of steps that morph and mix with each new phase you encounter. To complicate matters, your child will enter new phases unannounced and possibly off schedule from the children of your closest friends. And there is nobody out there prepared to tell you when the next phase will begin or if the current phase is close to ending.

Parenting is not for the faint of heart. It's not a place to experience unending freedom or relaxing moments. Parenting is HARD! But you know that already. You have experienced it up close, and you are ready for a little perspective. So let's get to it.

In the midst of growing little people into full-sized adults, failure is not an option. Too much is at stake. Great parents want more than mediocrity for their kids, and they believe the world should be a better place because their child has been added to the population. Helping kids to grow up to be influential and to be investors and contributors is the goal. That means you have to work hard, to have a growth mindset, to be willing to take risks, and to know when to stand your ground.

If you reflect on the purpose of your family, would you be able to articulate that purpose to others? Do you know why your family matters? Kids knowing and understanding their value is a direct result of how their parents instill that value. Beginning with the value of your family and helping members see their roles is a great place to start. If you were an organization, you might talk about what matters most or what goals you have. You might write down what you value or create a mission statement. If you could envision your household like that, what would you say is your mission? If you wrote down the purpose of your family, what would you say about it? Does everyone in your home agree with that direction?

Relationships are perfect for you to focus on when defining value, because they seem to matter more than anything else we teach our kids. If your mission is relational, you need to include relational training to help everyone in the family understand what matters most. To have successful adults come from your home, you need your kids to value people and the belief systems of others. You don't have to agree with someone to honor and respect him. That principle has to be modeled by you, inside and outside of your home, with consistency. You can model kindness, compassion, grace, care, honor, and respect, no matter how old your child is.

You will quickly discover that this book is not about *how to* parent as much as it is about *how you* parent and why. Theorists would have you believe that there is one ideal parenting style, but those theories were developed in the 1960s and may be a little outdated. Today, everyone parents to the beat of one's own drum, whether it is correct or not. Most people who want to know about parenting are looking for the answer to the question: "How?" The reality is that many of us don't really want to be told how; rather, we want to be patted on the back for a job well done. Regardless of how good of a parent you are, you are imperfect, and you parent imperfectly. There is no way to get it right all of the time. But don't let that give you the excuse to get it right less often than you should.

Education is another key talking point. Parents around the globe disagree on how education should happen. Most parents have idealized the value of specific educational systems from unschooling to over schooling and everything in between. We know best, don't we? But in your own home, it is essential to know that there is no better teacher than you. Your kids see how you handle financial windfalls and money troubles, relational highs and lows, moral and character challenging situations, and even daily routines. Your actions are more valuable than your words.

The world you grew up in is not the same as your children's, so it is imperative for you to shift your own parenting (or grandparenting) rituals to apply to the times. This doesn't mean you have to give up on your personal convictions; in fact, that would be a travesty. It means that you can show your kids how to stand up for what is right, speak appropriately, and communicate well. Help them learn to listen, show them how to be a leader, and expect them to be a follower, too. Help them learn that actions are loudly displayed, and that they don't have to speak to be heard. Help them learn to take turns, share, and be concerned for the needs of others. Help your kids learn compassion, grace, and mercy. Help them notice what is going on around them, and more than anything, teach them to be problem solvers. Help them understand that they don't have to be like the countless people who are waiting around to have their problems solved. Teach your kids to work, push on, keep moving, and to conquer demanding challenges.

You may wonder exactly what your role is, and this is it: Help your children to fall in love with Jesus, to care for others, and to become the adults they would like to be relationally. That means they need to learn to be friends, followers, and leaders at precisely the right moments. They need to become examples for the next generation, and when they experience pockets of success, celebrate with them, and celebrate your own hard work, too.

So how did you get to the place where you are today? Do you know why you make the parenting decisions you do? And have you ever considered how you could become a more effective parent? Follow me, and let's take a look.

2

The Parenting Void

IMAGINE WHAT LIFE would be like if you completed forty weeks of pregnancy, just as planned. The nursery was perfect; the name you had chosen was exactly what you wanted. No detail had been left unattended. You are ready for this new addition, and nothing else could be done to prepare you better.

On that day, you hop into the car and drive to the hospital. Make the setting perfect with a cherry-red sports car and your hair blowing in the wind. Take the time to stop for a selfie with your driver—the most wonderful life partner on the planet. Of course, you check your phone, but you already know the picture came out perfectly and posted nicely on social media as you announce your plans for the day. Hospital check-in occurred without a flaw, and labor was short and painless. Paint the picture as you wish, but remember, the day is magnificent in every way. The pinnacle moment has arrived, and the doctor has neatly wrapped up a blanket around your bundle of joy. You smile as you are handed a perfectly spectacular adult ready to go into the world.

Wait, what? You can't even wrap your head around this image. Why would you want an adult to enter your home like this? You would be so disappointed with the inability to shape his or her world or to invest your wisdom into this individual. Your influence would not be needed, and all of the stories you have planned to share are now simply useless. There would be no lessons to teach, no skinned knees to mend, no sleepless nights in the emergency room, no colorful casts to pick out, no braces to finance, and no eyeglasses to buy. There would be no ball games or tutoring, no homework, and no spilled milk in the minivan. You would experience no eye-rolling or talking back, and no broken heart or first date jitters. Can you imagine parenting without a single disciplinary action or redirected behavior? There would also be no prom tux to rent and no driving school to pay for. What exactly would be the point of parenting?

Instead, God has provided you with an individual full of flaws, full of needs, and with a desire to know you, to learn from you, and to bond with you. The journey is not easy, but if you are like me, you are quietly celebrating the current option. Raising kids is a far superior game plan than picking up premade adults from the delivery room.

At this moment, I challenge you to be grateful for the opportunity to shape this human who once arrived helpless and hungry. Do you love the tiny baby snuggles and coos that don't ever really go away? Do you cherish potty training, terrible twos, report cards, stubbed toes, and angry outbursts? Have you found the occasion to be thankful for the opportunity to be a coach, a mentor, a disciplinarian, a heart-changer, and a life-shaper?

The job of a parent may be incredibly hard, but the fingerprints you will leave on your children will shape their lives, will grow their world, and will change the next generation. Even better, they will help you to become a better person, and they will allow you to experience life from the role of a leader, a servant, and a caregiver. God delivers your children at the perfect time, with the perfect needs, and with the perfect set of elements already inside of them to become exactly who He wants them to be. Your job is simply to help them reveal who they will become.

Having worked with thousands of children and families through the years, I wish I could instill in you every bit of wisdom I have gained from their examples. In my own journey, I can remember wishing I understood my parenting role more. If I knew then what I know now, I am confident that I would have parented differently. The tiny details, the hard topics, and the emotional challenges I faced as a parent have prepared me to invest in so many others, and today it is your turn. My prayer is that you will grow, gain wisdom, and learn a little more about yourself as we continue to spend time together.

For you to be successful, your Parenting STYLE must involve a growth mindset, and though it will have its share of bumps in the road, you will be better prepared for what lies ahead. Inside these pages are tools that will help you assess where you are today, where you are headed, and what needs to happen before you finish. You might need to refill your coffee; we've got so much to talk about!

> *If we turn our kids towards others, when they grow up they are more likely to be the church than just GO to church.*
>
> —Adam Duckworth

3

The Desire to Parent Like a Unicorn

THERE ARE TWO kinds of people in the world—well, let's pretend that's true for a moment. When some hear the word *glitter*, it creates a harsh reaction in which they want to burst from the room to stay clear of anything sparkly. They can only envision the mess around them. And then there are those whose hearts cry with glee when they hear the words *shiny, colorful, sprinkle,* or *confetti*. Rainbows, glitter, and magical moments symbolize something just beyond physical reach, which incites them with creativity and imagination. Our oldest daughter is just that type of person. Her favorite color is glitter. The more it sparkles, the more she loves it.

So which are you? Are you a lover of shiny, magical, mystical substances, or are you a skeptic of the usefulness of anything sticky, messy, or glitter-filled? Few people fall in the middle, but you can take that stance as well. I happen to be a lover of glitter. I think it is because I won an art contest as a child—not because I was highly artistic, but because my art project stood above the competition as its shimmery three-dimensional lines sparkled amidst numerous others on display. All the other children drew their works, but mine had an extra element: glitter. We're not talking a little glitter, either. I must have used a few bottles of Elmer's glue to affix all that shiny attention-seeking bling. Love it or not, that blue ribbon at the art fair sealed the value of all types of sparkles into my heart.

Envision your daily life with me for a moment. Do you live for glitter-filled, ribbon-winning experiences? Among the mundane tasks of washing dirty dishes, folding laundry, finding french fries in car seats, reviewing report cards, helping with homework, and enduring sleepless nights, do you hope for moments that stand out among all of the others? I wonder if you wish for instances of social media bragging rights. Or do you wish others saw your life with more zing than it has?

For some, parenting feels like a competition. On one hand, do you love competitive moments that make you the superstar, and are you compelled to hunt for them? You might even be someone who plans them and articulates the need for them to exist. On the other hand, do you resent their very existence? Regardless of the presence of a bling-filled lifestyle, you still have parenting faux pas, and not every moment in your parenting journey is worthy of exhibition.

As humans, we love it when someone has taken the time to add a little sparkle to our lives, even if it is subtle. You may not love glitter, but you can appreciate what happens when someone adds a little something special into the world. It may not be as obvious as you thought, but how about sprinkles on doughnuts or chocolate shavings on cake? What about cinnamon sprinkled on

The Desire to Parent Like a Unicorn

the perfectly swirled latte or powdered sugar on a bakery treat? What about a beautiful paint job on that sports car you have been dreaming about—look closely: there is likely glitter in that paint. Do you love the beauty that embellished things have? Have you learned that just a little sugar on top of a muffin or sparkle on a superhero's shield can make the world a little more wonderful, at least for the moment?

Unicorns are mythical creatures that have recently made a resurgence into pop culture. Rainbow manes, sparkling tails, and glitter surround their single iridescent white horn. If you parent a girl, you likely have one within eyesight right now. Even teenagers have respect for the mythology of the unicorn. The majestic horse-like creature would be welcomed into your home if a live one stood on your lawn right now—and you wouldn't even think twice about inviting it inside.

If you could be the proud owner of a unicorn, you would be the talk of the town and the coolest dad at school. Your kids would be invited to every single birthday party. It sounds wonderful until you consider what you would need to feed it, where you would have to house it, and how you would have to clean up after it. But don't worry—it's not real, so those details don't really matter. Go back to your utopian thoughts of owning the one-of-a-kind beast that would make every parent in the world jealous as you would post photos on your social media page. Can you imagine if you owned a unicorn and received the attention that everyone is seeking, and that you just nailed it? You would have hypothetically won the proverbial parenting competition.

So much of the way we parent is like harnessing a mythological creature, inviting it into our home, and hoping for the best. Knowing that you are unsure of the details makes it more interesting but terrifying at the same time. The day you first brought your child home, your life was changed forever. I mean, REALLY changed! How could you love that creature so much and simultaneously wonder what in the world to do with it? The pathway to great parenting is not as mystical as owning a unicorn, but the uncertainty of the task is quite daunting.

For years, parenting experts have written books, explaining the chaos that occurs when green beans touch the tongue of a tiger-like child who was perfectly behaved thirty seconds earlier. Gurus have given wisdom on how to wrangle a cell phone from the fingers of an isolated teen, and theorists have explained why discipline does or doesn't work in any given scenario. Grasping that parent-of-the-year award is far beyond your reach, but social media eggs you on to strive for it, nonetheless.

The purpose of this conversation is much more introspective than most. It's a glimpse into your home and into your heart at the same time. It's a consideration of what is within your reach and what lies just outside of your grasp. Let's take a look at how you got to this point and question where you are headed next. Today you have a lot to think about as you actively reveal your parenting processes, the systems that you have created, how they got here, and why they matter so much. Ask yourself if

The Desire to Parent Like a Unicorn

you have any blind spots that need to be uncovered and if you have some belief systems that need to be brought back into the world of reality. You are not a unicorn, and neither are your kids. You will face unique situations, but many of your parenting duties fall into the world of consistency, modeling, and priority. Which of these three duties seems to be most elusive for you to grasp?

When you close this book's back cover, you will have knowledge that will help you grow and to work within your family support system. You will also have a plan for taking on the next hill, like a unicorn-riding knight in search of a dragon. You will be well equipped to tame any mythological beast—okay, maybe not that, but you will be better prepared to take on the next task you face, and you'll have a greater understanding of what your role is along the way. It's time to reconsider what is most important in your home right now, the phase your children are in, and what resources are available to make you the best parent you can possibly be.

Your family doesn't need to be broken or looking for answers to read this book. This journey was created for families of every shape and size. Whether you are parenting in a cohesive manner, struggling every day, or battling the tears as you read, you will find wisdom ahead. The journey will be fun, enlightening, and interactive—so let's get started.

Be patient. God is using today's difficulties to strengthen you for tomorrow. He is equipping. The God who makes things grow will help you bear fruit.

—Max Lucado

4

Understanding Your Strategic Parenting STYLE

IF YOU CLOSE your eyes and drift off into a parenting daydream, where does your mind go? Are you able to dream of well-behaved children, perfectly executed parties, and wonderfully attended playdates? Do your dreams include soccer practices, cheerleading camps, and painted masterpieces on the refrigerator? Can you place yourself on location for the pomp and circumstance of high school and college graduations, wedding bells, and science fair awards ceremonies? Is your child the next great musician, scientist, or athlete? Will your children live in outer space, own robots that clean the crumbs from their kitchen, or will they ever need to learn to drive? How is your children's world different from the one you grew up in? Can you picture yourself walking with your children through a garden and talking about what their adult years should be like? How will they parent or lead others? How will they make a difference in the world? What other questions should you ask?

Don't leave that daydream too early; your hopes are certainly valid. You will pass them on to your kids, either directly or through manipulative behaviors. How you see their future shapes the way you guide them. Your aspirations, your fears, and your resistance to specific outcomes are quite literally dictating who your child may become.

We will now talk honestly about the possibility that you may be having a hard time dreaming of a better family. You may be angry about where you are in your parenting, or you may have lost your joy. You may be lost and wandering, or you may have given up hope for your kids. I wish I could look you in the eye and tell you that everything is going to be okay. And I wish I could give you the perfect dose of encouragement to get you through today. My challenge to you is to stick with it. Don't give up. You are capable of raising your child, and you are capable of investing in the next generation. My prayer is that you can find a new perspective and that your introspective look at your parenting may reveal some areas where you can stand tall and face the areas that need to change.

When I was a kid, my parents never let me give up. If I fell down, wrecked my bike, or fell off of our horse, they urged me to keep trying. One summer, I did more belly flops in the pool than successful flips, but I learned that I was capable of flipping off of the diving board, and my determination to get it right helped me keep trying. There will be plenty of belly-flop parenting moments, but try, try again, and keep trying after that, too.

You certainly desire to see your kids flourish, and that desire is a wonderful driver, teaching you to invest wisely and rewarding you when you've gotten it right.

Understanding Your Strategic Parenting STYLE

Dear parent, please don't give up. Push through tough challenges, and stay the course.

When your children choose not to cooperate in the process of their own upbringing, you have hard decisions to make. You are the parent, and your job is to stick with them, motivate them, and challenge them to change their behaviors. You have to find motivational tools and figure out what works for each child individually. Parenting is tough, and keeping the right perspective is necessary to finish the task well. There are times you might choose to skip a step or two, but the formative years require some foundational experiences that can't be overlooked: crawling, walking, toilet training, spoken and written language, reading, self-care, social awareness, math, science, history, handwriting, texting, keyboarding, and so on. It's all a part of growing up. Skip the wrong thing, and you can see how that picture-perfect child in your daydream could be undermined. These are things that will challenge you to become better parents. These are the challenges that keep you awake at night. They shape your spending, your lifestyle, and nearly every choice you make. Parenting requires a series of decisions that either further the next step in the journey or squelch the possibilities and change the strategy of the overall game plan.

As a companion to this book, you will take a parenting assessment. It will help you see who you are, why you became that type of parent in the first place, and how you make parenting decisions every day of your life. Those decisions are your parenting strategy. They keep you afloat; they help you catch your breath before the next challenge comes to you. They direct you toward the next steps of discipline, control, cooperation, and communication. They are critical, and they are what make you the best parent you can possibly be. Parenting strategies are what help you to do more than just survive; they help you thrive or at least attempt to finish the course strong.

Your parenting STRATEGY is derived from components involving more than one parenting STYLE. This strategy may be really obvious to you, or it may be a completely new concept. Your mind reasons that you parent the way you do because of the components of your strategically balanced lifestyle. If that strategy lacks intention, there may be pitfalls ahead.

To understand your strategy, you need to understand why you use it. If you are in your best place, you parent one way, but when you are at your worst, you tend to parent at your worst. So you have an imaginary scale in your mind, and it wants to overcompensate for the bad by adding a little extra good whenever possible. Your reasoning may mislead you to believe that a little good can erase a lot of bad. Juggling your inner self, your own parents' voices, and the influences of others, you have adopted the parenting STYLEs you have simply because you believe they are the best fit for your family. It's much more complicated than being authoritative, authoritarian, or permissive—like the parenting styles you've been exposed to in culture. In essence, you are not just one of those, but you also have a complicated blend of parenting that allows you to shift, change, morph, and dodge your fears, and you have developed those skills

Understanding Your Strategic Parenting STYLE

through a complex process. You have lived through relationships with others and attempted to influence your kids because of those relationships.

Without making it too complicated, there are several weight types that can be on the scale in this assessment. They are a balance of your parenting skills, the good, the bad, and the less than wonderful. You may see one or all of them on a given day, and you may depend upon them for different reasons. But you go to them to help you fulfill strategic plans you are making about your child's future. Let's take a look:

- Your TRUE STYLE—This is who you really are when nobody's around. There are no secrets hidden in your TRUE STYLE; this is genuinely you oozing out, for better or worse. Your kids may know your TRUE STYLE better than you do.
- Your REVERTED STYLE—This is what you return to often. This is what you're good at, what you enjoy, and the parts of parenting you don't have to work at. These seem to come naturally. The danger is that this can be a lazy zone or a style you revert to when you want to take the easy route. Caution: This style may keep you from facing the hard decisions you need to make.
- Your AVOIDANT STYLE—This is what you fear doing. You parent in this zone because you don't want to appear to be something you despise. You AVOID becoming your parents or AVOID becoming THOSE people. You know you are

living this style out when you catch yourself being something or someone you never wanted to be.
- Your HEALTHY STYLE—This is where you should be. This is not the guilt-ridden, uncomfortable, made-up lifestyle that is imposed upon you by social media or the expectations of others. This is what you know is right, what is good and wholesome; this zone includes the right amount of balance in every aspect. In some regards, this is unattainable all of the time. But when you're living the HEALTHY STYLE, you know it, and you know it's right.

Have you ever noticed the similarities between life and getting your hair cut? You have to make an appointment, travel to get there, wait your turn, climb into a chair to wash away the residue of the day, switch chairs, have a safety barrier put around your clothing, close your eyes, sit up straight, and be prepared with a plan before you even start. You have to trust someone else to finish the vision you have, and if you are lucky, it all comes out as planned. When you look at the hair-covered floor, you feel as if you've paid to have a part of yourself removed, but when you look in the mirror, you realize it was all worthwhile. The actual test is when you can style it yourself the next day, or if you have to wait for two weeks before it feels normal again.

The parallel to life is astonishing. When we need to fix something minor, it isn't noticed as much as when complete makeovers are required. After our third child was born, I cut off all of my hair. We're talking about 16 to 18 inches of long, thick curls. If you have as much hair as I do, you see the value of this conversation much more than the person who simply needs a trim.

Maybe you routinely cut your own hair or simply shave your own head. You might feel that you are able to cheat the haircutting system a bit, and you might take that same approach to life: "I'll just cut it all off or I'll just do it myself." But you can see the difference when a skilled hair artist has completed the task instead of an untrained pair of hands. You have seen the results when a four-year-old's dull scissors come in contact with her bangs. And you have seen the results of a nervous mother who used clippers to save a few dollars, but the back of her child's head is proof that this was a bad idea.

In what areas of your life are you trying to fly under the radar in a do-it-yourself approach? Is anybody noticing? It is essential to find skilled, wise counsel to invest in your future when it comes to parenting. Would it be advantageous for you to find a qualified parenting specialist to help your family deal with improperly attended family matters? Have you ever considered that you don't know how to handle the current parenting situations you are dealing with because you have never done this before? Let's dive into the questions, the reasoning, and the life experience that brought you to parent the way you do.

Five Key Components have developed YOUR PARENTING STYLE:

S—STABILITY as it has been instilled in your own life; your foundation. These include your upbringing, traditions, religion, and relationship with your parents, and the investment by others in your youth.

T—TANGIBLE EXPERIENCE that has taught you wisdom and understanding. This is where you have learned through pain and gain in your own life, and you pass it along to others around you, especially your offspring.

Y—YOURSELF. You are human and you are social and emotional. Your aptitude for social and emotional experiences determines how you will manage stress, chaos, and the unknown, as well as how you will connect with others through the good, the bad, and the ugly.

L—LIFESTYLE is determined by your resources. Finances, assets, or the lack thereof have a significant bearing on your family's ability to have and to obtain. How you focus on what you have and what you value determines how your children assign value. This can drive expectations and most definitely changes how you are viewed by society.

Understanding Your Strategic Parenting STYLE

E—EXPECTATIONS should always be managed well, even your own. Morals, values, interactions, and boundaries shape your expectations of yourself and others. Simply stated, EXPECTATIONS determine the outcome.

You don't have to be a perfect parent. You are required to have only a certain amount of knowledge, and you'll never be an expert at everything. You might be great at changing diapers and terrible at limiting screen time. You might be excellent at helping your child read and terrible at helping him get his shoes on the correct feet. The great news is, many people are in your life who are also parents, and they may be able to help you at just the right moment. Their experience will help you manage your own expectations so you can become better at the things you are good at while working on the things that need attention.

Just like a haircut, you have to set aside time intentionally, you have to consider what needs to change, and you need to commit to the process of becoming the right parent for the right phase of life you are living in. There are a few things you can do on your own. Start with your relationships. Your relationship with God, spouse, and children are important for your success. Your parents, your extended family, and even your in-laws will shape your future and the future of your kids. Invest in these relationships, and in turn, they will help to invest in you. If you naturally tend to nurture relationships, you are already a step ahead of the game. If you have wonderful family connections, take a moment and consider the significance of that support system. If you have less than wonderful relationships with your family, consider what it might take to get those relationships into a better place. How could you be instrumental in bridging the gap where it is lacking?

Once your kids have left home, you will realize the significance of the relational investments you have made. The most important relationship to work on is the one you share with God. When you learn to rely on Him, you will see the other relationships come into place. My suggestion is that you start there. Ask God: What area of my relationship needs a little work today? What area of my life needs a total makeover? How can You help me to become a better parent?

5

Parenting Imperfectly

I PUT THE key in the ignition and looked carefully in the rearview mirror, then the side mirror, then the other side, over my shoulder, and back in the rearview. I drove forward, then back, forward, then back. I turned the steering wheel to the right and pulled ahead, aligning the wheels perfectly straight. Then I backed up. Nope, that wasn't right. I pulled forward again and turned the wheel left. No matter which way I turned the wheel, and no matter how quickly or slowly I backed up, the trailer turned in the wrong direction. After thirty minutes of frustrating silence and building blood pressure, I asked my husband to park the trailer. He pulled forward, looked in the rearview, the side view, the other side, and over his shoulder. He pushed the gas pedal, and both the truck and trailer effortlessly parked between the lines. I closed my eyes for a few seconds, let out a disgusted breath, and walked away. My stubbornness didn't fix the problem, and despite every combination of solutions I could find, I could not park the rig correctly. I was grateful that my husband parked the trailer, but I never tried again.

Take a deep cleansing breath, savor the oxygen for a moment, and think about the perfect parenting experience. A deep sigh might escape as you dream about the last time you slept through the night or ate a meal without whining voices complaining about the food you just spent hours preparing. Take another deep breath and think back to the last meal where you didn't have to clean up a mess, do the dishes, or react to a waterfall of spilled milk on the table. Can you remember the last phone call without interruption or the time you went to the bathroom with nobody around? There was that time you had a complete conversation without bodily noises or eye-rolling interrupting your train of thought. Can you remember it? If you are a parent, you know how hard it can be to find a few moments alone or feel that you are in control. Take one last deep breath and know that parenting is hard, but you are doing great.

Is your parenting like my trailer parking expedition? Do you find yourself trying the same wrong approach over and over? Do you need someone to help you figure out what needs to happen next? Have you ever been so stubborn that you couldn't let go of the wheel? Some of those hard parenting moments get us stuck because we can't seem to see another solution.

You arrived inside the parenting arena with less than a year to prepare for the magnificent, complicated, beautiful addition to your family. How could you have known it would be this exhausting? Why didn't anyone warn you about the loss of privacy and the lack of sleep, or how much it would change absolutely everything in your life? Some people became parents in a very short time, but forty weeks is the typical experience. That was probably the last time that your parenting was remotely framed as typical.

From the moment that tiny bundle entered your world, life has had a way of taking control right out of your grasp. And though you plan to get every detail right, textbook parenting is less like reality and more like a fairy tale—it's just not realistic to think there is a single plan for success. Whether you got here today through foster care, adoption, marriage, assisted or natural means, parenting is a journey that has more unexplained moments than you could have ever predicted.

I volunteer with an organization that offers mentorship for teen moms. I'm astounded at the challenges that parents face today. These young ladies amaze me at the responsibility they take on at an early age! I have learned so much watching them navigate a pandemic, diapers, teething, and schooling, all while parenting (in many cases) alone. My kids are grown, and though there are some differences in the world they grew up in, post-COVID parenting is just as challenging as it was post-9/11. The reality is, parenting is amazing, wonderful, beautiful, messy, unpredictable, and incredibly HARD! No two people parent the exact same way, and by design, parenting was not intended to be a do-it-alone task. Regardless of how you parent, when you parent, or what started your parenting journey, there are some similarities worth discussing.

Hop onto any social media platform, and you will see beautiful pictures of ideal families dressed in matching pajamas with perfect hair and beautiful homes. You'll be tempted to desire their lifestyle, even though you don't know what they have quietly tucked outside of view.

You will dream of being like the parent whose child has perfect grades, has all the right friends, has just finished potty training, or has just gotten a full-ride scholarship. Keep clicking, and you'll see parents laughing at their kids' mess and showing off their crazy lives. Swipe to the left, and you will see parents asking for prayer because they need help or because their child is sick. No matter what others post, you really never understand their complicated lives. And no matter how hard you try, you don't have the ability to fully grasp all that goes through your mind as you momentarily compare your broken pieces, wins, and befuddled moments with theirs. "I wish I were...," "I'm glad I'm not...," "I hope someday..." phrases cross your mind as you try to relate, but closing the browser doesn't answer your questions or solve your problems. It just helps you know you're not alone.

Where is your loneliness? Where is your strength? What is going great in your parenting journey? Today, you are standing somewhere on the hypothetical parenting scale, staring at the number between your feet and wondering if the display shows that you are healthy or you need to enhance your parenting routine. You are on an invisible spectrum that ranges from zero to 100 in some unknown dimension. Some days, you are the judge who determines the score; other days, it is your child's teacher, your friends, social media trolls, your parents, or your children themselves. And somewhere in there is a real number that could be determined if you look closely enough. What is your parenting score? How would you be doing if you gave yourself a grade today?

Parenting Imperfectly

I like the idea of measurement; as a teacher, I understand that performance can be measured, which indicates learning and skill. It shows aptitude and possibility. Educators never administer a test for the sake of testing; they want to see the data it provides. If someone created a test for parenting, I don't think it could be as simple as pass/fail or 0–100. Life is way too complicated for that. The scale would have to include your care, courage, leadership, decision-making skills, ability to juggle a thousand tasks simultaneously, and even your best recipe for macaroni and cheese. If someone wanted to assess everything you do as a parent, it would take years just to compile the probabilities. You're busy, and your life is changing every single day. Sometimes you wonder how you fit it all in, and you're confident that nobody else could do what you do.

Just for a moment, let's consider the top and bottom ends of the scale. It might be more fun if it were defined in animal nomenclature. The worst animal I can think of is a cockroach, so we will place "roach" at zero. The magical, mystical perfection known as a unicorn will be placed at the top, right beside A, or 100 percent. Now consider where you fall on the cockroach-to-unicorn scale. Give yourself some grace, have a little mercy, find some extra credit points somewhere, and don't judge yourself too harshly. I bet you fall somewhere north of the middle and somewhat below sparking glitter unicorn.

If you have a partner in this venture, where would you place his or her parenting? Research in the United States indicates that less than 50 percent of parents score themselves highly when defining success. Fewer than 50 percent of parents feel they are doing an excellent job or feel confident that they are leading their families well. Less than 40 percent are confident that they know how to handle the next disaster ahead, and less than 25 percent are confident they have what it takes to successfully raise a child from birth to age eighteen.

You don't have to feel as if you're failing when you admit that you don't have everything figured out in parenting. Relationships with other parents help us to keep our feet on the ground. I'm not talking about the comparison game, but about healthy relationships where you find support, share ideas, and encourage one another. Once you find these relationships, if they are healthy, you will find imperfect parenting stories. Other parents have have less-than-ideal situations and heartbreaking experiences to express. You will also find partnership, camaraderie, and fresh ideas that will provide opportunities for conversation and food for thought as you embark on today, tomorrow, and next week.

As your child enters the next phase or closes out the current stage, you will need to change strategies and prepare for the journey—it is part of your success story. This means finding other parents to join your circle of influence, which is a critical decision to make. If you have those relationships, keep them well oiled and be sure you are giving as much as you are taking. Stop right now and text those individuals and thank them for their role in your parenting experiences. Their voices matter.

Parenting Imperfectly

There is no date set on a worldwide calendar in which your child will learn to walk, talk, run, read, date, or talk back, but those events are coming to your home, whether you are prepared or not. Your child has so many complicated components that you will never be fully ahead of the game. And if you have more than one child, the game gets even more complex. Give yourself a break, the permission to fail on occasion, and some grace in the moment. Even better, afford these opportunities to your friends and family. Our culture offers judgment so quickly and gossip so readily, yet we need support from one another. I've learned that when I begin speaking with humility, my friends share similar stories. They have also had difficult experiences and were too embarrassed to talk about them.

In an attempt to become a unicorn parent, you may have gotten really good at hiding the bad and displaying a persona of unrealistic expectations. There is danger in perfection—your kids need to learn to become adults, and they need to see you work through your own problems, challenges, frustrations, and failures. If you are the perfect parent, the perfect spouse, the perfect employee, the perfect athlete, or the perfect Christian, your kids will never fully comprehend grace, understanding, forgiveness, or reconciliation. Those are key areas of their development, and they need you to model those successfully, but they also need to see you model them imperfectly. They will learn when you admit that you have completely made a mess and can't figure out how to undo it. Kids need to see both healthy conflict and resolution in action.

They are watching, and your life is as much of a teaching tool as your words.

There is a fine balance between perfection and false expectations. The physical and verbal examples in your actions and your language are noticed. If your mouth is negative and full of hateful words, your kids will notice. If you speak only sweet words and kindness, your kids will see that, too. Your actions can't be faked. Be sure not to set false expectations for your kids, and do not be inconsistent between what you say and what you model. Help set your kids up for reality and realistic expectations in all of the relationships they will encounter.

It's imperative that the other influences in your children's lives are consistent with your expectations. You are building a village of voices in their lives. They need people who will help them make sense of hard times. They need voices that speak into their world when they reach the age when parenting decisions don't always make sense to them. Consider carefully whose voices are given center stage. Think wisely about who needs to be included in critical conversations. Become strategic as you involve others in your children's lives before problems arise.

Contemplate who can help them learn things that you are not good at. Concentrate on those who will say the same things that you would. Help your children's circle of influence to become strong. Help them know there are others they can turn to, even when you are not around. And give them permission to have conversations with others in that circle when they need a confidant, a friend, or a second opinion. Widening the circle of influence will make you a better parent.

*When you want to prepare your kids
for life in the real world, focus on encouraging
their heart to be in relationship with God.
God will do the rest.*

—*Isaac Giles*

6

Parenting Perspective

WITHOUT EVEN SIGNING up for the competition, you have become a contender for any and all parenting awards. Without accepting the challenge formally, you are in the great parenting race to become perfect, though your life is anything but. In this century, there is a very real, very public battle that masquerades as friendliness. The cutthroat parenting competition you are somehow a part of doesn't stop at reasonable measures, and I doubt it would end if someone achieved unicorn status. Instead, the challenge to win at parenting makes every other part of life less meaningful. It makes it a full-on race to a never revealed finish line. And when someone else appears to be getting ahead, it is easy to start the comparison game. It is possible to sling mud, to attempt to show off your own unicorn skills, or to try to one-up the competition. But parenting isn't a competition. Your children aren't little trophies to be displayed in your family room or posted on your social media site. Children are a gift from God, even when they don't feel like a blessing. However, if everything goes as planned, you will have less than a thousand weeks of influence from the time they are born until they head off for college or into their adult lives. In fact, if you do the math, there will be 936 weeks between your child's birth and age eighteen. That means you have a very short time to mold your children into the adults they need to become.

We started this book with the story of your child being a kid first, not an adult. And if your journey is already underway, consider if you may have missed out on some influential moments. My prayer is that you will commit to making future experiences filled with inspiration and influence. Even if you didn't have a Christ-centered childhood experience, or that hasn't been the initiative in your home before today, it's not too late to start.

As God gives you a child, He equips you for the job of parenting. He gives parents the privilege of helping mold their kids into the adults they will become. My friend Alicia shared with me, "It was hard for me to grasp the fact my kids are His children first. Even on the days that I don't see them as a blessing, they are His blessing to me. As a parent, I have to remind myself that I need to do better by and for my kids, because first they are His children."

Knowing that your 936 weeks are underway, do you feel the pressure to fill each day with the most you possibly can? Are you like Alicia? Do you see your kids in God's plan? Do you see His role in their lives?

Time is of the essence. You have character to shape, education to instill, nutritious meals to plan, and physical and mental health to juggle. You will deal with technology, exercise, and relationships with friends, family, classmates, and even romantic interests. You'll face fashion and poor eating habits, bullies and playground battles, pimples and deodorant, birds and the bees, and

Parenting Perspective

difficult situations such as bike riding lessons, driver's licenses, proms, graduations, and sports. Your child needs music lessons, moral teaching, and religious experiences to fit into that handful of time, not to mention sleep, three meals a day, and time to read a little before bed. The pressure to do it all perfectly is hard enough, and managing the weekly schedule makes the entire endeavor feel next to impossible. You need a healthy perspective of your parenting journey.

Have you ever thought of yourself as a professional parent? You are. You are an expert. If you have experience, you have something to share. You don't actually get paid to be a parent, but it is your job, and that makes you a professional. From that perspective, you should act like a professional. You should know your role and live it with passion. If this were your career, how would your boss guide you? What would your next performance review look like?

Brian and his wife Isabelle were very aware that Ryker was not walking or talking like other kids, and he was not as tall as his friends at daycare. They spoke with their doctor about his physical challenges and insisted that medical tests be run to prove nothing was wrong with their sweet fourteen-month-old son. When Isabelle picked Ryker up from daycare, she was given a piece of paper stating he couldn't return. He had bitten another child. Isabelle began screaming at the caregiver and blaming her for not paying enough attention so the action could have been stopped.

Isabelle wasn't very professional, and her anger was projected in the wrong direction. She felt out of control, and she had fears of not being a good mom. Ryker's actions were not unusual for a child, but Brian and Isabelle had been consistent in their approach to being good parents, and this felt as if they had failed. Our kids have behaviors against what we want and expect, even if we have the best intentions and perfect parenting processes.

Though many people may never understand your specific challenges, they are very real. Others may look into your glass house and wonder why you don't see some of your parenting flaws. They judge, criticize, and question your parenting choices. There is a danger in caring too much, and there is a danger in dismissing input altogether.

Growth can happen when others critique us, but everyone must know which voices to listen to. Just as I have challenged you to surround your kids with wise voices, the practice is good for you as well. It's good to hear others warn you of cliffs you don't see, twists and turns ahead in the journey, and things you are simply blind to.

Parents who choose to ignore something obviously wrong with their child are making a mistake. But often, they don't want to admit that their child falls outside of what would be considered "normal." There is a fear of failure when your picture-perfect family has a flaw, but the truth is, every family has flaws. It doesn't mean you have to post yours all over social media, and you don't have to flaunt the challenges you face. Just as in other areas of parenting, the word "balance" applies here.

It's a great idea to ask your inner circle for support. Be sure to balance the amount of information you ask of others with being a problem solver for yourself. You can often solve a problem if you are willing to invest the time and energy to put into the solution.

If you post a question or a brag moment, balance the negative social media with the positive. Balance the rose-colored-glasses view of your children with 20/20 conversations with friends. Ensure that you are not projecting unrealistic expectations on yourself, your child, or your friends.

Sometimes I walk away from a conversation wondering why a parent addressed me with an issue. Sometimes it's because I am willing to listen, but often I don't have the answer a parent needs. Today, I spoke with a mom who was completely overwhelmed with her six kids, and she asked me what she could do to get their attention. I love this question, but if I didn't have a big family, I might not have been able to answer. When you share your heart, be sure to ask the right person. You don't ask your dentist how to cut your child's hair, and you don't ask your mechanic how to groom your dog.

Here are some areas worth discussing with someone who has already been there or survived:

- Understanding learning delays
- Hygiene practices that kids don't like
- Bullying—when your kid is the bully

- Bullying—when your kid is being treated badly
- Mean girls
- Poor grades
- A teacher who is missing the mark with your child
- Your child's angry outbursts
- Laziness
- A child with addiction issues
- When to talk about the birds and the bees
- Character issues (tattling, cheating, stealing, etc.)

The list could go on, because asking for wisdom is natural.

The purpose of such a conversation should be about how you can be a better parent to a child with a particular struggle. It's easy to see how our kids should grow, but as parents, we should be growing just as rapidly. Every parent strives to be a lifelong learner, but being a continuously growing individual is even more critical.

Parenting can be lonely. You can feel isolated right out in the open. Having healthy conversations leads to a remedy in that loneliness. Relationships can make you feel better about yourself, or they can tear you down. Finding healthy, growing relationships will help you grow. That means you can dig in and isolate yourself when you feel you are failing or struggling, but that's usually the wrong way to move forward. Trusting someone you can talk to, finding a friend who is struggling with the same issues, or seeking out someone just a step ahead in the process can be helpful. Part of self care is your own mental health, and you know you are headed in the right direction when you are growing and not staying the same or moving backwards.

Inside healthy relationships, you lean into your shortcomings and look for the right answers—not just easy ones. And inside those friendships, you can discover that transparency helps aid your growth experience. Be sure that you are open and honest. I've learned that people often explain 90 percent of a problem in business and ignore 10 percent. As a parent, be sure to uproot the whole issue and not just the top 90 percent. The nitty-gritty hard work comes in the 10 percent that you really want to cover up. It will turn into a negative cycle of repeating problems if left alone.

Consider a dandelion. It's fun to blow the white seeds around, but the plants are difficult to uproot from your lawn. Your child may enjoy getting into trouble, but the real problem occurs when one bad action grows into multiple behaviors, just like dandelion seeds. You can pick the cute little dandelion flower and even pull the prickly leaves from your lawn, but unless you uproot the portion of the plant that is underground, it will continue to grow. You might not see it for a few weeks, but it will be back. And interestingly, this time it will have even more flowers present.

Consider your child sighing deeply when you ask him to take his plate to the kitchen. He lingers a little, shuffles his feet, huffs and puffs, comes up with an excuse, and finally makes it to the sink where he places the dish, which should have gone into the dishwasher. You pick up the dish, rinse it, and put it into the rack. You've picked the flower and asked your child not to do it again—but there is more going on here than an unwashed dish. How will you deal with this once and for all? How will you be consistent to ensure this little challenge doesn't become a big one? Do you see the multiple issues to address here, and not just one?

I can't stress enough how important consistency is in parenting. What other parenting challenges might you need to discuss with your friend, your group, your mentor, or other wise individuals in your life?

Here are a few to consider:

- Your anger
- The words you use to let your child know his behavior is unacceptable
- Your tendencies to favor one child over another
- The buttons you allow your kids to push
- Your disdain for _____ (behavior)
- What you don't like to see in other people's children and how to control your shortcomings so you can model good behavior for your kids
- Double standards you may have
- Your mental health challenges that limit your parenting capabilities
- How you can take care of yourself better so you can care for your child better

You see how your parenting challenges may not just be about your child's behavior. Consider what dandelions you are breeding right inside your home.

Parenting Perspective

In the second chapter of the book of Luke, you can read the well-known story of Jesus' birth. And suddenly, the writer changes from talking about angels, swaddling cloths, and a stinky stable and answers a critical parenting question. Imagine being there in that space with Jesus' parents and asking them, "So what are you going to do with that baby?" Verse 52 tells us what their plan was. Jesus grew in wisdom, in stature, and in favor with God and men.

- Wisdom—He grew in mental knowledge, education, and logic, and in learning to use wisdom.
- Stature—He grew physically and in strength. He became a healthy adult.
- Favor—He grew in relationship with God and with people.

Jesus had to grow in his relationship with God, and so do we. Luke says, "Love the Lord your God with all your heart, mind, and strength." Luke goes on to show us what favor with man is. He said, "Love your neighbor as yourself" (Lk 10:27).

Mary and Joseph prepared Jesus to know everything He needed as an adult. This provides a little insight into their parenting, and it is great wisdom for parents to consider what really matters most.

When it comes down to it, there is no perfect parent, no perfect parenting plan, and no handbook for parenting success. But here are a few guidelines that will help you lead your family into a healthy lifestyle:

- **Be authentic.** You don't have to be perfect, and your kids want you to be real.
- **Honor God.** This is the most essential step. Expect everyone in your home to respect God and each another.
- **Teach your kids to rely on God.** A relationship with God matters to you, and it should matter to them as well, but depending on God is an even bigger challenge. He's got this!
- **Treat others well.** Model this for your kids so they see that all people matter, all people should be cared for, and all people deserve their goodness.

Mary and Joseph had the perfect child, and yet they had a job when it came to parenting. They had three simple words to guide them with raising their family: wisdom, stature, and favor. How will these words shape your family today?

You became a parent as a result of your choices, influence, and decisions. And mixing your identity with that of a child can be more challenging than you think. Just sit back for a moment and consider how much thought you put into parenting. Consider how hard you have worked to make it right to where you are and how badly you want to become a unicorn. The struggle is real, and sometimes you add pressure by trying to juggle too much. It's hard to be a taxi driver, medical doctor, counselor, and chef while being perfect in your own job, your own social life, and your own relationships, all at the same time. No amount of education can prepare you for every twist and turn, but perspective can sure make the journey more enjoyable.

Perspective. Just sit with that word for a moment. Take the word and let it sit in your hand and look at it from the top, bottom, side, and back. Are you looking at your life with the right perspective? How about your child's life? What really matters most? How would you define success for your child? Is that the perspective that should drive everything? If not, what is the proper perspective?

I love the word "expectation." I use it with my adult children, and I introduced it to them when they were preschoolers. I have expectations of each of them, and they are different in general for each child. My kids couldn't be more different, yet I feel God equipped me to be their mom and walk the journey with them, in front of them, beside them, and behind them. My perspective changed every single day, but expectations never have. Three expectations top the list: (1) Never give up—try your hardest and never give in; (2) allow your influence to be managed correctly; (3) and always make the wisest choice from the options you have available. We often asked this question in our home: "Is that what God expects from you right now?" It helped our kids gain a perspective and to become introspective about their priorities without us pointing out problems or nagging about unfinished tasks. Teaching kids to allow God to be their compass is one of the most important tasks we have.

Don't compare your behind-the-scenes with somebody else's highlight reel.

—*Steven Furtick*

7

Parenting with a Growth Mindset

SOMETIMES WE CHANGE, and we don't even know why. We don't have to announce it for others to know it has happened. Sometimes we want those changes to be covered up, and other times we want people to notice.

Have you ever had a favorite donut shop, coffee spot, or ice cream stand? One day, you change your mind and turn your car into a new drive-thru, and you're hooked on a whole new flavor. For the time, that new treat is your go-to unnecessary calorie spot, and you like it that way. Those new changes get you out of a rut and often broaden the horizons of your treat consumption. You tell others about them as if you have climbed the Mt. Everest of coffee spots or tackled the greatest mystery of all time. It may be just a new treat for your 4 P.M. cravings, but it is yours, and it is fantastic.

Ice cream flavors, trendy snack foods, and caffeinated beverages can help illustrate how your ideals can change, but you are much deeper than that. You have had fundamental, profound, conviction-led life changes as well. How you model change for your kids is a big deal. They need to learn that your opinions can change in healthy ways. They may be forced to change, or you may desire the changes. But being flexible enough to change is only the beginning. Among the most challenging types of change you can model for your kids are adaptability, flexibility, and resilience. Teaching kids to adapt to the demands of the moment is crucial for adult living. And for your kids, learning to make those decisions when you aren't around is paramount. Being flexible and resilient can't be overlooked as you prepare them for the future. For you to set them up successfully is complex parenting material.

The hardest part of being a parent is watching your kids go through circumstances in which any or all of their ideals are challenged. If you stop reading this book today, don't miss this thought: The more your kids work through at a young age, the more they will be able to work through when they are older. Let's frame that correctly. Your kids will face challenges, and if they learn to overcome, they will be overcomers. If they learn to cheat, they will be cheaters. If they learn to blame, to be lazy, to avoid, to hurt, or to complain, those things will continue to be lived out in their lives until they tackle them. The most important thing you can do for a child is to encourage them to work through the tough stuff and not to bail them out. Of course, that must be age-appropriate, and it doesn't mean they need you to add to the pressure. They will face enough opposition in the world when they simply need you to be their coach, their greatest cheerleader, and a safe guardian as they embark upon new and challenging situations.

You are a safe guardian for your children when you ensure they have what they need and they know how to respond. They are protected from harm, but they are not protected from learning experiences. Like a lifeguard, you watch over and protect your children, even in troubled waters. Allowing your kids to swim in the deep end is important. Be that lifeguard, prepared to throw a lifeline in times of trouble, but don't save them from every rocky current. Those experiences will strengthen them and prepare them to be better swimmers when the water becomes even deeper.

Growth happens for every child in different areas. That's what is great about being human—we will all live different lives and will face different problems. For kids, growth is required, and parenting requires an acknowledgment that they will want to run from struggles, but they will experience them nonetheless. Their battles will be unique compared to some friends and similar to others. There will be a first day of school, a first date, a first broken heart, and a first boss. There will be a first fight, a first skinned knee, and a first bloody nose. Help your children know how they will respond, even before an event occurs. This proactive approach will help develop their character for any future experiences. Each experience they encounter will help them to grow in their ability to deal with the next. You may understand their problems, and you may not. You grow from struggle as well, and your kids may not understand that in the moment of pain. Help them to learn that all of our relationships grow from struggle. Allow them to feel some tension and to make decisions inside that tension. Don't always give them the answers. Give them safe places to fail, and coach them through the tough decisions. Ask them, "Is that the wisest thing to do right now?" Offer your children moments to contemplate their actions and the repercussions. You do not have to know exactly what your children are experiencing all of the time. Sometimes it is helpful for them to sit in that struggle and give them space to problem solve. In this area, they transform from helplessness to problem solvers. The less they need you to solve their problems, the better.

In the natural order of the world, God has provided all people with growth opportunities. Growth happens because of survival and successfully dealing with various aspects of the challenge at hand. It happens inside of challenging moments and due to difficult situations. Growth occurs in spite of everything we contribute to our children's world, and in every place that we neglect to support them as well. A growth mindset requires you to look for positive outcomes. That means teaching your kids that the giant ahead can be conquered when facing an obstacle. Still, having the mindset of improvement, a philosophy of success, and a lifestyle of perseverance must be taught for your children to be ready to use their giant-managing skills when needed. Kids must gain the ability to find perspective and an understanding of their battles. They need tenacious skills to press on through tricky situations. They must acquire a toolbox of competencies that come from practice under pressure. Parents must be instrumental in teaching these skills and introducing truth. These are the tools needed to take on a challenge and beat the odds, and for kids to be successful.

Americans love a comeback story. Hollywood has filled our movie screens with heart-wrenching experiences where someone beat back the odds and came out victoriously. Have you ever gotten a little emotional in the theater? Your heart aches while watching the character's despair and rejoices when he wins. You cheer for the overcomer—even if only internally, so nobody else in the theater notices that lump in your throat or the little tears welling up in your eyes. When you begin to see the light at the end of the tunnel, you move to the edge of your seat. But those individuals would not have had the opportunity to flourish if their mom or dad stepped in and solved the problem for them. Let's have a little fun with that thought.

Imagine George Washington's mother standing on the side of the Delaware River with a pair of shoes and some hot cocoa as the men got off the boats. Right in the middle of the war and heroic action, a mom's hot apple pie and warm hug would seem lovely. But the strength and endurance your history teacher taught you about those men would be diminished. Mary Ball Washington could have changed history by taking away the heroic nature of men without gloves and hats fighting a freezing cold battle to win freedom for the masses. Today, proud Americans wouldn't look at the seriousness and the sacrifice they made. No one would have paintings depicting their tenacity and courage. Honor would be lost. Would they have been seen as heroes without the stamina and ability to press on against all odds? What picture would you conjure up when thinking of the famous scene? It would undoubtedly change if it weren't so monumental and if the grit and tension were erased.

How about this one: Imagine if David's mom and dad told him not to go to the battle to kill the giant Goliath. Of course, they should have been concerned for his safety, but the entire history of the Israelite nation would have been different. If David had put on a helmet and pads, he might have been safer, but he proved his bravery and heroism because he took on the impossible and won, not because his parents helped him solve the problem. I think David's parents had already instilled bravery, exposed him to decision-making situations, and allowed him to discover the usefulness of slingshots and other tools as weapons. They helped him be prepared by polishing his curiosity for what was happening in his world and allowing him to understand the seriousness of the situation. Don't you love that his parents taught him to rely upon God and to trust God's plan in action?

Here's another one: Imagine if Tony Hawk (the famous skater and X-Games champion) had a parent who taught him ballet instead of skateboarding. If his mom or dad had told him not to flip his bike upside down or stop doing dangerous things with his skateboard, he would not have gotten the practice that revealed his talents.

Critical thinking is such an important skill, and kids need to be proud of the good decisions they make and understand the bad ones, too. How would the ending have been different if Muhammad Ali's mom stopped him from fighting and punished him every time he came home with a black eye? I'm not saying you should encourage your kids to fight, but consider what would be different if you prepared your child for making decisions, facing tough challenges, and working it out when things didn't go as expected.

We love stories where things get better in the end, but even the great leader Martin Luther King Jr. thrived in a world of adversity. Though his life didn't end as a parent would want, his life was valuable, and his actions made the world a better place. What if MLK's mom told him not to be so outspoken or not to preach to others? Would his life been so influential?

By no means should you neglect your children's decision-making process when they go in the wrong direction. You must guard their hearts when they desire to experience a thrill that is out of control or display rebellious attitudes when they are turned in the wrong direction. The purpose of this discussion is to consider your perspective. Are you over-thinking your parenting? Are you stepping into too many decisions your kids should be making for themselves? Are you doing things to help your kids that are actually removing learning opportunities from their world?

If your kids are too young to make their own lunch, ride their own bikes, or do their own laundry, tuck this concept away for that chapter of your journey. But remember, even children just learning to walk may need to learn some independence from you. Inside the safe place you have created for them to grow up, you have to gauge how often you are willing to let them miss their intended target before stepping in. Your home must be a safe place for them to fail because they need you to coach them toward success. They are practicing being adults, which means they aren't perfect. So as they gain confidence, choose independence, explore capacity, and stand on their own, you must also learn how much separation is appropriate at a particular age and stage. Separation from you requires wisdom and balance so they will know that they are ready for you to let go. If your child can accomplish something independently, make it a rule that you will never do that for them again.

You can see how parents could stop all kinds of behaviors that are considered risky, but in many cases, these types of actions have changed the world. Your influence in your child's life may well prepare them for something incredible. The way you handle it today may affect their future and their influence, possibly for thousands of people or for many generations. Your choices matter, and sometimes the easy thing, the safe thing, or the most logical thing is not the choice that will help your child practice using their growth mindset.

Your perspective must help nurture growth in your children. Wise decision making and the ability to operate inside any given structure, even when you are not around, is the posture that will help your children succeed. This is what we call a growth mindset. Your kids need to learn to grow and to find growth opportunities. Teach them to love living a strong and fulfilled life and to desire better things for themselves. Teach them to discover what brings satisfaction and fulfills their personal goals. Challenge them to separate this from selfish ambition and manipulative thinking.

In your quest to become a unicorn parent, there is a shifted reality ahead. You will gradually shift all of the responsibility you carry onto your children's shoulders, so they can become the adults they need to be and can thrive in the world.

You have countless voices influencing your decisions, individuals casting their judgment, and the need to wisely discern what comes next. The journey is yours, and you have the ability to help your children be exactly who they are intended to be, and your inspiration could make all the difference. You've got what it takes, and you are capable!

<u>PERSPECTIVE CHALLENGE</u>:

This week, while you're in the car or at the dinner table, ask your kids about a famous person and ask how their story would have been different if their parents stepped in. Would it have been better or worse? Why?

Of course, the list is endless, but here are a few to consider:

- Joan of Arc
- Henry Ford
- Queen Elizabeth II
- Michelangelo
- Amelia Earhart

- Abraham Lincoln
- Gabby Douglas
- Milton Hershey
- Rosa Parks
- Neil Armstrong
- Sally Ride
- Nikola Tesla
- Harper Lee
- Herschel Walker
- Deborah Sampson
- Jeannette Rankin
- Morgan Freeman
- Helen Keller
- Usain Bolt
- Rosalind Franklin
- Eleanor Roosevelt
- Houdini
- Jane Austen
- Stan Lee
- Anne Frank
- Paul Revere
- Shoeless Joe Jackson
- William Shakespeare

8

Directionally Challenged Parenting

SO YOU'RE NOT a unicorn? I didn't expect you to be perfect, and everyone knows that you aren't. This is a great place to start. So what animal would represent you better? Monkeys are my favorite animal to observe. They are curious and a little crazy. They are acrobatic, and they are resourceful. But I can't say I would like to parent like a monkey. I tend to gather the family for projects, ask the kids to work together, and celebrate as we accomplish tasks. I think an ant is the animal that fits my parenting journey a little better.

Isaac and I have been married for more than thirty-two years, and we had our first child just eighteen months into our marriage. Kurt and Olivia Bruner (Heritage Builders) challenged us to make intentional parenting decisions very early on, much like picking up a compass, reading the heading, and moving toward an intended target together. It may be the best marriage or parenting advice we have ever received.

I'm going to assume that you know how to drive. If you are a parent, you must be able to get back and forth to appointments, to work, and to social gatherings, and I'm going to assume that you have, on at least one occasion, had an unsafe driving experience. Of course, you are a perfect driver; it is those other people around you who don't know how to drive.

In full transparency, I must admit I am directionally challenged. I would probably not survive in the forest if I got lost hiking. I am a landmark driver, and even the best GPS fails to tell me to turn at the red barn or drive past the gas station on the corner to get to my location. East and west were simple while growing up in a mountain state. I learned to drive toward the mountains or away from them. But when we moved to the East Coast, I lost my sense of direction. It was probably never there, but I didn't know that. I am grateful that my phone and car both have GPS capability, because it is often required to get me to the correct location.

The choice to move in a specific direction indicates movement with a purpose. A compass, a GPS, and the right set of tools help the traveler to stay on the marked trail. Parenting can be filled with distractions, and like a directionally challenged driver, you can get lost easily. Keeping your compass in hand will help you take each step with destination-directed intention. Parenting requires that you find your due north and stay with that heading. If you swerve off of your path, it may be difficult to re-center.

Have you ever had that experience of your trusty GPS spinning just at the moment you need to know which road to take? Or, like me, you have had to make a U-turn to go back to the missed exit on your route. You see how the analogy fits with parenting. A single misstep can be detrimental, but if you act quickly, the possibility for a U-turn is often present. You rely on technology to get you there safely and on time. Wouldn't it be wonderful to have a GPS for parenting? How often would you hear the words "recalculating, recalculating…"?

If you move in a single, predetermined direction as a family unit, you can experience life together. For us, it would have been chaotic to live as six separate individuals walking through the world aimlessly, hoping to reach our intended destinations – not to mention traveling without a plan. I love the GPS analogy, and I love that it made us parent together and become intentional about our parenting choices. It brought my husband into the decision-making role as well. We began to observe a considerable deficit in the presence of other dads in our group of friends and wondered if we could help men to join in family decision-making. Often moms make the decisions, and dads become the enforcer of behaviors along the decision route. And we observed that when dads make decisions, moms must pick up the slack to make them happen. But we didn't find many of our friends picking up the family compass and talking through the intentional movement needed to move the troops from point A to point B in unison.

I can't imagine feeling the weight of parenting entirely on my own because I've had a great partner in the journey. But each day, I walk alongside moms and dads who are taking the journey alone; whether they are married or single, they experience parenting without a partner. If you are in that type of situation, I want to encourage you that it can be done. I love that you are reading this book and looking for ways to improve. I am confident that in spite of your best skills, you can't parent alone. You may find more unconventional means to build the support system for your children to grow up in.

Give voices to mentors, babysitters, grandparents, friends, and church leaders. Immerse your children in a system where love comes from others besides yourself and where encouragement, life lessons, and even guidance through tough decisions happen through multiple voices. No matter your living situation, your children need other voices saying the same things that you are, teaching things that you can't, or reinforcing things that you've already taught. Part of being human is living in a world of people, and your children need to learn their places in that world from you and from others, right from the beginning.

No matter how many voices are in your children's lives, the compass trajectory must remain the same. You have some decisions to make. What kind of adults do you want your children to become? What voices and directions need to change for your children to reach the right destination this week, this month, next year, as they turn eighteen, as they enter their first jobs, as they choose relationships, and as they lead their own families? Are there any influences that need to be extinguished or whose volume should be turned down? Are those voices leading your children toward God or away from Him? Have you been clear in your intentions with those who speak with your children? Do they know your expectations for them to help your children move toward some solutions and away from others?

Our oldest child became defiant when we removed a familiar television show from our home. She was so connected with what that show was teaching her, and even at two years old, she depended on that voice more than what we desired. It was an uphill battle but worth the fight. Looking back, I see that we removed an influence that was not in alignment with our family values.

One last thought on the compass: There will be a time for you to pass your compass to your children. They will need to know where they are heading and how to know when they are not on the right path. You will need to prepare them for the task of re-centering and the long journey ahead. As you know, there is no single destination in life that is labeled a success, and your children need to understand that morals, values, life practices, and decisions should be their anchor, keeping them from drifting too far. You can only give them the tools they need and teach them to use the compass. If you are a safe-parent type guardian, the guardrails you have put into place can be explained to your children with love and logic. As they become adults, you will see them get it wrong, struggle with reading the compass, and then redirect. This is precisely the time to encourage them the most.

If you are struggling with the concept of a compass, consider morals, values, rules, or guidelines that your children should learn for direction. They should begin to form a conscience that will guide them even when you are not around. A biblical worldview is one set type of compass. A moral foundation is another. Regardless of your spiritual habits, teaching your child how to distinguish right from wrong is critical.

I speak with many empty nesters who struggle with their role after their kids have left home. If you are an adult and your parents are still trying to act as your GPS, ask them to hand over the device. Plan well ahead as you parent your kids through this transition and consider just exactly what that will look like. I doubt the handoff will be like a baton in a marathon. I think it may be shared ownership for a time, maybe during their last year at home. And perhaps it will be more abrupt, but partner with your kids to know when each one is ready and mature enough to take on that life-owning role.

9

Culturally Independent Parenting

OUR CULTURE ENCOURAGES independence, and while that is a great thing, understanding the purpose of autonomy in partnership is also critical. Autonomy is the ability to control yourself enough that you can be trusted to work within fewer parameters. "I want to make my own decision" is often confused with "If nobody is telling me what to do, I am free." Freedom comes by earning the right to be free. Freedom is not a gift to be entrusted to someone who doesn't know its value. The individual with fewer people telling him what to do is the person who can manage his affairs with less direction. That means that self-control, self-government, and mature thinking are needed to reach a place where freedom can be given.

If a child wants freedom, it should not be given until he is able to practice the principles of self-government without parents managing the situation. Independence can be confused with freedom. If I want independence, I want a lack of controlling power over me. That's not the same as having control. It is crucial for kids and adults alike to understand the link between autonomy, freedom, control, and independence. They are partners, just as individuals must partner in each of these areas to ensure they are managed correctly. If a parent lets go of control, that doesn't mean a child is in control. The child must choose to self-govern and show he is capable of control. Parents and kids are the partners in this conversation, and parents must take the leading role.

Just one ingredient makes this recipe successful: the self. One must care for others more than oneself. If you wonder if you are ready for an autonomous experience, here are some questions: Can I be trusted? Can I act wisely? Can I be just? Can I use logic? Can I use restraint? Can I see others, care for others, and honor others inside my own free experiences? Am I responsible for my own life in ways that I can transfer into other settings? Do the needs of others have value in my decisions?

Here are some questions to ask if you think your children are ready for independence: Are they able to be trusted? Will they make wise choices? Will their actions reflect what they have been taught? Can they use restraint? Will they actively care for others as they work through this experience? Does anyone else need to help them make good decisions?

Total independence is not actually independence at all. It's kind of a mystical thought. There will never be a time in life free from all demands, all requirements, all instruction, and all expectations. Helping our kids understand that maturity includes knowing how to handle situations and how to self-govern will help them learn to cooperate well with others and be good life partners. This will transfer to friendships, business, and family relationships as well.

Culturally Independent Parenting

If your children learn that only one person makes decisions—AKA you—they won't learn to make reasonable choices. If they don't experience a lack of authority, they will not learn the freedom of operating well under authority. If they don't experience situations where they must show respect, honor, gratitude, thankfulness, care, kindness, mercy, grace, patience, and even peace, they will not know their value.

By diminishing their children's need to make decisions and to choose wisely, parents stunt their ability to grow. Having a growth mindset means parents must allow their children to make decisions, feel repercussions when they fail, and manage their lives inside and outside of controlled situations. Lack of independent thinking can reduce your children's ability to work well in society. Teaching independence is great, but teaching kids to work within parameters leading to freedom and the ability to make choices is a much stronger position for parents to take. Helping kids learn respect inside of dependence will help them learn respect in times of independence and prepare them to make wise decisions throughout their lifetime.

Have you ever groomed a horse? I would imagine that grooming a unicorn is similar. Let's go with that. After you go on a ride, it is vital to cool the horse down, walk him around a bit, brush his hair, and ensure no foreign objects are inside his hooves. In fact, horse experts suggest cleaning the hooves every day. Removing debris, making sure that infections are not able to start, and looking for problems are all reasons to clean the hooves. A horse will also bond with the individual who cleans his feet. He'll come to depend on that person, and he will know the caretaker is helping him.

Parenting is not just about keeping your kids looking great for the sake of appearances; it is also about bonding with them as you help deal with the debris that could potentially harm them if left unattended. Bad habits, inappropriate interactions, or childish behaviors are best dealt with immediately and not allowed to stay unattended. And let's face it: if we want to be unicorn parents, we should have the best care and treatment ever. That means attending to the bad as well as the good.

10

Parenting with a Support System

KEEPING MY HOUSE clean has been a challenge with raising four kids, caring for pets, and working full time. My husband is a saint for all of the laundry and dishes he has helped with over the years. Not only has his partnership in life been fantastic, but his partnership in parenting has been priceless. Everyone in the family knows that Dad has different cleaning standards than Mom. I can remember the kids asking, "Does it have to be *Mom* clean or *Dad* clean?" Sometimes I chuckle at their questions, but I'm glad that my kids know the difference. There are times in life when you need to rise to the occasion and meet a different set of standards. Our kids need to know the difference.

Healthy relationships are two-sided, and modeling that for kids is essential. No matter what your past experience looks like, I would encourage you to find a person who can help you to weigh difficult decisions and to discern wisely, and who can be there when it all blows apart. Nothing ever goes wrong at opportune times, and because of that, you need a person or a support system before a crisis happens. That person needs to know when your parenting method is the best and when you need for them to step in and help.

My husband has learned that there are times to ask me to help the kids with cleaning, and I learned there were areas in which he was a better help to them. It's not just about a spouse or a single partner in your life who helps you to do things the best way possible. Your family also needs to know where to get help outside of the walls of your home when necessary.

A few weeks ago, I received a phone call that sent my heart racing. Our adult daughter had been in a serious car accident, and I needed to leave work immediately. I was able to reach out to my support system as I made the twenty-five-minute drive. My thoughts had gone everywhere you could possibly imagine as I worried about what I would discover upon my arrival. Previously, our four kids have had terrifying medical situations, bad car accidents, and embarrassing moments, and I am so grateful to the friends and family who have supported us in those times.

Our third child had more opportunities for us to build our support system than our other kids. One night, he showed us his finger that needed emergency surgery, and another day he fell while setting the table and stood up with a fork parallel to his nose—and embedded in his forehead. He later had something surgically removed from inside of his nose. For the next emergency, he was hospitalized from smoke inhalation after our stove caught fire. There have also been many other times when

Parenting with a Support System

family and friends have actively provided the support that we needed.

Who is in your support circle? And who helps to shoulder the challenges you face in your parenting journey? If your system is adequate, have you stopped to thank those involved? I wonder if your support system needs to grow or if you should help carry someone else's parenting weight. The more kids you have and the more adventurous they are, the more opportunities you will have to allow yourself to be supported.

I once heard a sermon encouraging everyone to be both a giver and a receiver and to do this well. It takes a conscious effort to be a contributor and not just a taker. I love that challenge, and it's something I've taught to each of my kids. Every relationship affords you an opportunity to serve others or to be served, to love others and to be loved, to care for others and to be cared for, and to grow in your relationship as you help your partner to grow as well. Humans need one another, and along the parenting journey, we all need to remember to be as supportive of others as they are for us. Teach your kids to rely on God, to connect with people, and to build healthy relationships. Model this for them daily, and you will see this growth in every corner of their lives.

I'd like to take a moment and talk about the most important relationship in my life. My relationship with God has changed everything about me. I am grateful that I am not the person I was yesterday, the day before, or the day before that. And I'm so grateful that I'm not the person I was in college or in high school. God has helped me to grow and to become more of who He wants me to be. He is the third partner in our parenting decisions. He has created the lens by which value, character, success, and priorities are measured. And I simply can't imagine life without His presence. He is not just my copilot—He directs my life. My relationship with Him is my top priority. I am confident that faith comes first, family comes second, and everything else comes after that. Those priorities influence everything I write, and I challenge you to consider where God's influence is in your life. Your support system is not complete without a personal relationship with God.

Nearly every part of our support system is involved in a religious community. I would encourage you to find a church, find friends there, begin relationships with people who share similar values, and get involved in a community that worships God. You'll be amazed at how quickly your support system grows. And if you have a life partner who attends church with you, his or her support system will grow as well. It's incredible how the presence of people shapes our own values and those we instill in our kids. The church is a great place to begin.

By now, you have taken the Parenting STYLE Quiz, and you realize that your parenting style aligns with an animal. We did that for fun and to help you discover how you interact like other creatures on our planet. Imagine if every animal in the jungle was helping to support your child. I lovingly refer to my kids as monkeys because of their curiosity and daredevil acrobatics. Even as adults, I sometimes catch myself picturing them as young and

Parenting with a Support System

adventurous little monkeys. What animal would you say best represents each of your children?

In an attempt to help you better understand your own personal parenting experience, this assessment has been created to pair you with a specific animal on the roach-unicorn spectrum. Don't worry; nobody ever achieves the title of a unicorn here—and that's not even the goal. Your Parenting STYLE is something fun to explore, and as we have begun to talk about navigation with your parenting compass, you have seen how your STYLE has helped you so far and how blending your STYLE with your support system can help set you up for even more success.

Most people don't have just one Parenting STYLE. You might make great decisions when you're operating inside one style, but when you're in a bad space, you might parent from another. And we've noticed that some may parent in avoidance of one STYLE more than intentionally into another. We'll talk about that a lot more, but if you haven't done so, stop here and complete the online Parenting STYLE Assessment. We encourage you to have everyone else in your inner circle complete it as well. It will take less than thirty minutes, and you'll have lots to talk about when you're done.

Your greatest contribution to the Kingdom of God may not be what you do but someone you raise.

—*Andy Stanley*

11

Understanding Your Unique Parenting STYLE

UNIQUENESS PLAYS OUT in your parenting. There are so many variables in this conversation; you will never parent like anyone else you know. In a way, that is really special, and in another way, you may discover it catches you off guard.

Are you an animal lover? I intentionally avoid any type of pet store, dog pound, or humane society. I would want to take home every animal I see, and I would regret that choice before I ever got out of the parking lot. The pets at our house know that they can ask for treats, request playtime, or go on walks just by locating me when they want help. When we go to other people's homes, I can't help but talk to the dog, pet the cat, or go with the kids to meet their rodents.

But God didn't make all animals the same. He made a type of creature called a snake. I have no words to express how much I don't enjoy snakes. Touching their skin is like scratching a chalkboard. Looking at their eyes is like staring at the sun during an eclipse. I've never figured out why I loathe snakes to this degree.

I'm willing to bet that there is an animal that you don't like and that you wouldn't want it to represent you.

What animal would you choose if we created an emblem to illustrate your parenting style? It would be fun if all parents had to wear identifying shirts to the park and we could see who is a badger, a mouse, a bat, or a horse. I bet we would find endless reasons parents selected those creatures.

You have discovered your parenting STYLE, and you identify with a certain animal. So now that you're a _____ (enter your top identified Parenting STYLE animal here), what does that mean? You will not parent this way 100 percent of the time, but a lot. In fact, it's more likely to be between 70 and 80 percent. There are both positives and negatives in each STYLE, and we will explore what happens as you become more self-aware. We know that you will change your approach in parenting decisions as your children grow up, and you might even find yourself parenting from different STYLES along the way.

Your Primary Parenting STYLE is the one that scored the highest. It has become your top set of stylistic choices because of your own upbringing, your resources, the time you have to invest, your personality, your expectations, and your partnerships. In the pages ahead, you will discover why these matter.

Let's start using the word IDEAL instead of PERFECT. In an ideal situation, you have the ability to make a difference. Since there is no such thing as a perfect situation, the expectations of UNICORN kids and UNICORN parents are erased. The expectations you place upon yourself and your support system are now in a more realistic perspective.

When you have unrealistic expectations, your Parenting STYLE might be more defined by one of these words:

- Over-involved
- Overwhelmed
- Overachiever
- Obsessive
- Compulsive
- Guilt-driven
- Manipulative
- Rebellious
- Avoidant
- Angry
- Neglectful
- Forceful
- Shaming
- Indulgent
- Over-permissive
- Under-equipped
- Resentful
- Blinded
- Failing
- Humiliating
- Fear-filled
- Controlling

How would life change if you replace those words with these:

- Growing
- Improving
- Intentional
- Adjusting
- Thriving
- Valuable
- Stable
- Balanced
- Partnership
- Blended
- Supported/Supportive
- Successful
- Age-appropriate
- Confident

There is a difference between saying I AM A SUCCESS and I AM SUCCESSFUL. Which of these phrases best fits your parenting today? Reframe the question and make it more realistic. You are not expected to be perfect or even successful all of the time, but you are a successful parent, even when the wins are tiny. Having a growth mindset can occur when you believe you can improve and when you want to be the best you can be. You have tools, strengths, and a support system to help you move into a thriving growth-mindset Parenting STYLE. And if you have the privilege of having a best friend, spouse, or life partner that joins you in this journey, your chances of raising a successful and thriving adult suddenly multiply.

So just who is it that defines parenting success? I hate to tell you that there's no real answer to this question. And there is a big difference between unrealistic expectations and reality. You've seen the Internet memes that feature what others think of you and what the truth is. My friends think I'm terrible at parenting when my child cries, my mom thinks I'm terrible at it when my child argues, I think I'm a superhero, and my kids think I'm crazy. The reality is that nobody is actually right. Perspective doesn't change the definition of successful parenting. But please don't let those words give you an excuse to neglect your role as a parent. Consider what is age-appropriate, what expectations others have of your kids, and how they are being viewed by their peers.

I was having coffee with my friend Jen, who began describing a misbehaving child. She was stunned by how another friend's child could be so repulsively defiant. It was so bad that Jen had planned to skip her granddaughter's ballet performance, as this defiant child would be dancing there as well. Additionally, Jen and her husband were considering giving up a Christmas tradition event with all of the grandkids because she knew the other child would be present at that event, too.

I asked Jen why she didn't speak to the parent about the child, and I listened as she described an even worse situation. Just one week earlier, the mother and child were in the grocery store, and he picked up an apple and took a bite. The mother put the apple in a bag and placed it in her cart. The child opened the container of free cookies for kids in the bakery section and touched many cookies before taking one out to eat. The mother just closed the container and walked down the aisle. At the checkout, the child opened a candy bar and began eating. The mother put the candy on the conveyor belt and paid for it. Never once did the parent say anything to the child about expectations. The mother simply paid the price and did nothing to keep it from happening again.

It's no wonder my friend was uninterested in being around an unruly child, but it is astounding to know that the parent had no intention of redirecting the child's behavior. This is an opportunity for a great conversation in your home. Just how much should a child be allowed to operate outside of society's expectations before something is said? What is the appropriate way to approach a friend whose child is on a path of destruction?

Before you begin to give the mom a pass and say that her child would eventually figure it out, I want to provide you with an important detail: this child was seventeen years old. Take a moment and process that. How would this scenario be different if the child were age two, four, or even five? This story isn't about casting judgment; it is an opportunity to reflect upon what your child is doing that is not age-appropriate. In what areas do you need to require your child to work harder or break bad habits? It might even be an opportunity for you to ask a friend to be transparent and give you some feedback on your parenting and expose the blind spots you have.

12

Your Parental Job Description

THIS STORY IS much like our parenting. With our oldest child, permission was necessary, and then she quickly took over in many areas of parenting. Our second child learned to stay out of the riff-raff and settle for less than perfect, but not to cause a fuss. Our third child always pushed against the system, and our last child always knew he could get away with things the others couldn't. Does birth order influence your home? Parenting was different for all of our children because each responded uniquely to various situations.

There are times in life where we have to face situations that don't really make sense. You may be blamed for something that wasn't your fault, or you must deal with the consequences of someone else's behavior. As a parent, you may have opportunities to experience this with your children.

A few short years into our marriage, we rented a townhouse in the suburbs of Denver. The home was an excellent place for our growing family, but a job change made the commute longer than we wanted. We moved to a condo closer to work and were awaiting the return of our security deposit from the landlord of the townhome. Much to our dismay, we got a bill from the landlord. Apparently, the carpet had been damaged and needed to be replaced. In those pre-cell phone days, communication was primarily through snail mail, and photos showed a perfectly round bleach spot in the middle of the dark brown carpet. It looked like the rings left after a wet five-gallon bucket sits on concrete.

As we were leaving the townhouse for the final time, the landlord was hauling in cleaning supplies in a five-gallon cleaning bucket. We had left the place in great shape, and we wondered why he was arriving to clean. There was no way to prove that his bucket had caused the damage, so we lost the money we were counting on. It didn't matter that we knew the truth; we had to pay for the damages. Needless to say, the cost of that situation was quite a setback for our little family.

As we talk about your Parenting STYLE, what setbacks have you had that were unexpected? What events came up that caused you to respond, even when they didn't make sense? Have you had to deal with any situations involving your kids that were not your fault, even though they appeared that way? How could you have handled them differently? Consider the situations from your past that set you up to handle the unknown. What experiences left you unprepared for parenting? Is there anyone who would help you take a closer look? How do the expectations of others change your parenting? How do they limit your ability to move forward?

About two months before our first child was born, I felt a sensation in my abdomen that was much different from the usual. It repeated, and I got excited, then scared, then excited again. That feeling that the baby would be here soon was a great reminder that our family was changing, and I needed to take inventory of what still needed to be prepared.

The afternoon moved on, and so did the contractions. I walked around a little, but they didn't change. I had read so many books that I was a birthing expert—or so I thought. I decided to call my doctor, and he was a little concerned that I was earlier than he wanted me to be. The moment he suggested we go to the hospital, the entire scene changed. Full panic mode set in, and my very calm husband became a person I had never met before. He had prepared an overnight bag without my knowledge. He grabbed the keys and was nearly out of the driveway when I made it to the car. Two wheels touched the ground as he rounded the first corner. A cartoonist could have animated the scene well as we drove fifteen miles in a much shorter time than legally suggested. The wheels screeched as we arrived at the front door, and my husband was quite shocked with how slowly the staff moved. I was in labor, and he needed them to act quickly. Once my vitals had been recorded, things slowed even more. The nurses were nice, but nobody was in a hurry. Only ninety minutes had passed when the nurse smiled and said, "Well, the good news is, this is a false alarm."

Thankfully, the drive home was much more controlled, and calm was back in our house as we went to bed. On the day our daughter was born, Isaac drove to the hospital and met me there. No police escorts or sirens or screeching brakes were needed. The labor was long and generally routine for the staff. Everything was pretty much textbook until the moment they handed me our baby girl. All predictions indicated that we were having a boy, and I can still feel my shock when the doctor announced her gender. We were once again unprepared for the next step in our parenting journey. Thankfully, we had considered a girl's name. But that was about the end of our pink-ribbon-and-lace preparation.

It took me a few days to remove the blue overalls and baseball caps from the dresser and replace them with purple bows and pink dresses. I kept a few warm baseball sleepers and football items. She looked cute in those, too. Have you ever noticed that some of your best-laid parenting plans are interrupted by people who don't consider them as urgent as you do? Or people who wonder why you are so worried about little things like footballs on a little girl's pajamas? Sometimes the real priorities are missed among the urgency we create around them.

We should have seen the blessing in the nurses and doctors who were not in crisis mode when we arrived. That was a sign that we were in good hands and the situation was not serious. We should have seen the beauty in having the ability to switch gears even though our child was not who we expected to take home with us. And we most definitely should have been focused on the healthy child that arrived without any severe labor conditions. Our own urgency to have a baby who fit all of our checked boxes could have derailed our family if we had allowed it.

From the moment you are expecting, there is an imaginary parenting job description that you begin to seek.

Your Parental Job Description

There are tasks you can list and ones you could never put into words. There are simple arrangements such as researching every possible website, buying the latest *Consumer Reports* magazines before ordering the safest car seat on the planet, and more complicated tasks such as holding your child the first time she throws up or gets a shot. No matter how prepared you are, you will never be perfect, and you will never be able to compile a list of all you need to accomplish in the parenting years. So let's talk about it from an ideological viewpoint instead. You will be responsible for each item on this hypothetical parenting job description, and somehow you must decipher what those jobs are. This is not the ideal world of parenting, and there are many more tasks than you ever estimated. Just when you think you have arrived at the finish line, it might move. Your kids will never be perfect and neither will you. Though social media expects you to be a superhero, you can do only the best you possibly can—some days, even that is a stretch.

Once upon a time, you may have believed the goal was simply to bring your child into the world, but it is much more complicated than that. You spent forty weeks preparing, reading, and planning the perfect birth experience. You might have even taken a birthing class. But helping your child come into the world was only a tiny piece of growing him or her into a successful adult.

That is what you are doing after all: helping your kids practice being adults. The more you teach them, the more you set them up for success, and the less you do to get in the way of that progress, the better off they will be. There is a lot to teach them, a lot to guard them against until it is age-appropriate, and a lot to consider every step of the way. There will be times you're wrong, times you're frustrated, times you'll completely mess it up, and times you'll experience the worst imaginable outcome. But there are also times of triumph, celebration, growth, encouragement, and winning. The most outstanding parenting achievement is not seeing your children grow up; it is seeing them become the people they are intended to be.

God has a plan for each person, and as parents, our role is really about coaching our kids to fulfill His plans. There you have it: the real definition of parenting success. Comb through your hypothetical job description and consider what you should add or take away from the phase you are currently in. If you are parenting a toddler, you aren't worried about talking back. If you are parenting a teen, curfew and friends might be on top of the priority list. Just as you would consider your job description at the office, take time to consider how well you are doing here. If you were giving yourself a quarterly evaluation, would you get a raise, be written up, or be fired on the spot?

What stands out most? What adjustments do you need to make? What areas do you need to let go of? I challenge you to ask your kids, friends, and spouse. Taking time to reflect on your parenting is much like getting a report card. Don't beat yourself up, and don't quit—you and your spouse are the only parents your kids have. But let the reality be motivating for the next quarterly assessment, which is just ninety days away.

13

Parenting Effects

FALL IN NORTH Carolina is absolutely breathtaking. We made the decision to move here during a family vacation just as the leaves were changing. Driving through the mountains with gold, red, purple, green, and every shade of brown, the beauty of creation fully engulfed the sky with a canopy of branches that were dusting the road below our car's wheels.

As we drove that day, the majestic trees were every shape and size, and the colorful leaves looked like confetti at a parade. I began sketching the scene when we got to our cabin, and I thought about the strength of a tree that stands tall beside the road. Under the ground, its root systems must be robust to hold up the weight of the trunk and withstand the wind as it rustles through the leaves. I contemplated the weight difference a tree experiences as it begins dropping the beautiful foliage on the ground. I considered the relief a tree branch might feel as the weight is lessened.

Each year the tree grows more leaves, gains new bark, and gains a bigger trunk. The spread of the branches is more prominent and the reach is farther. The majesty of a tree comes with age. A tree that grows above the ground is also growing below. The root system is expanding, and the entire structure is sturdier. The species of the tree and the environment play a significant role in the tree growth process. Some trees will never be as big as others. Some will have yellow leaves in the fall, while others will have red. Some will bear fruit, while others bear cones or needles. And every tree has random characteristics.

Many people believe that tree root systems mirror the branches that are seen, but in reality, the roots spread out and are flatter under the surface from what is seen above the ground. Another interesting fact I discovered is that an injured or broken tree can compartmentalize a section until it heals. And trees can grow back strong after an injury.

I hope you see the simplicity of this analogy. Families grow in every shape and size. They may look beautiful at times and less attractive in other seasons. Just like trees, there are too many types of families to name, and every family has unique features. And consider for a moment how vast your family's root system is. As your family grows in strength, it isn't a majestic structure in the beginning. That takes time. And the longer your family is together, the more it is seen by others. The fruit you bear is different from that of others. My favorite detail is that your family can heal, even after serious situations threaten to destroy you.

Your family tree is a symbol of legacy, strength, and something that should last through time. How will you pass that on so the next generation adds to the majestic structure just as you have? How did your parents and grandparents prepare you for the leadership role in this stage in the life of your family tree? If your current family tree is not the legacy you want to pass to your children, what changes do you need to make? What are your plans to alter it for the next generation and improve the structure for them? You can be the one to make that change, and you can start right here—today. It will take intentionality and effort, but it can be done.

Understanding who you are as a parent, right here in this space, will help you understand your children's trajectory. Chances are, much of what you are teaching them will show up in their parenting as well. The way you punish them, reward them, challenge them, encourage them, and even the way you nag them may have ripple effects far beyond this moment. Psychologists spend much of their time unraveling parental absence, shame, guilt, anger, rejection, and abusive situations. But they also untangle manipulation, addiction, unrealistic expectations, and unhealthy boundaries that parents have imposed either directly or indirectly upon their kids.

Though you're never going to get it all right, it's a good idea to attempt to get most of it right. When you don't, be the first to apologize. Model that for your kids. Help them begin to see healthy relationships and boundaries in their relationship with you. You are not their friend; you are their parent, and it will help them if you establish that line carefully.

The majority of parents dream of having the perfect relationship with their kids. It is tricky to know when to protect, when to challenge, when to discipline, and when to offer grace. Either way, modeling reality, realistic thinking, and real-life experiences will help your children to be prepared for their own real-life decisions down the road. They don't need to solve your problems or be involved in all of your choices, and they certainly don't need the power to make decisions for your family. They do need to see that you struggle with some of those things. They need your leadership and your wisdom. They need your discernment and your best decisions to be on display.

I recently spoke with a dad whose three-year-old had decided where their family was vacationing. I met another mom who makes two dinners every night—one for the adults and one for the kids. I spoke with a dad whose eleven-year-old son chose the new sports car he bought in lieu of a family minivan because it was more important for him to be dropped off for school in a cool car than one that could hold the whole family. I talked with a sixteen-year-old whose mom described her dating adventures to him, and the conversation grossed him out. Another parent recently shared with me that her son doesn't clean his room well enough, so she does it for him—and he is nineteen.

You see how inappropriate some parenting decisions are, while others may seem benign. Kids should be kids and should not be making grown-up decisions. They shouldn't be your support system, and they shouldn't be part of your inner circle of friends. They need to be well respected and must be expected to respect you. Their needs and wants should be weighed along with other family members, and in that scenario, no one person should ever dominate.

Sometimes kids need to hear the words NO and WAIT. If you find yourself sacrificing day after day for kids who seem to be growing more and more selfish, it is time to reconsider the source of the problem. If your children are running your house, it is time to stop letting them. Kids are bright, and family meetings are a great time to set up or reestablish rules.

As kids grow, they can take on more responsibility. They should help with chores, and if they are capable of a task, you should never be the one to do it. Packing lunches, putting away toys, cleaning their bedrooms, sorting laundry, and putting away groceries are things even young elementary kids should do.

As we dive into your Parenting STYLE, you will see a snapshot of where you are today. Your strengths and weaknesses follow the information in that particular Parenting STYLE. Your Growth Mindset Parenting STYLE will look different from others', but take a few minutes to consider what parenting choices you should be more aware of and notice what problematic situations you may encounter. Be wise and learn before you fall into the great parent trap.

In the mid-1960s, Dr. Diane Baumrind introduced a baseline set of parenting styles used by psychologists and professionals around the globe. Her assessment measured the control and warmth of parents and provided guidance that promotes being an authoritative parent. Setting boundaries, building self-esteem, and nurturing kids typically sound great. Still, there are three other parenting styles on her list: Permissive parents who give kids too much autonomy, authoritative parents who are too demanding, and neglectful parents who simply check out.

Through the years, others have contributed the terms "helicopter parent" (over-involved), "tiger parent" (highly defensive), "hovercraft" (never letting go), "over-indulgent" (never says no), "screamer parent" (never stops yelling), "control-freak parent" (fears everything), "hypochondriac parent" (always thinks his child is sick), "ski-lift parent" (just wants to get the children to eighteen and out of the house), and many more. It's easy to fall into parenting pitfalls, and as we explore your family dynamics, you may see some of your own poor habits that need to be uprooted.

That's a really healthy place to be. You may find that you need to talk with a mentor, a pastor, or a counselor to move forward. Your family is not like any other, and your stressors are unique. You may have some baggage from your own childhood that you are bringing to the table. But don't forget to take a few minutes to count your blessings and celebrate them as well. Your home, job, support system, children, spouse, and relationship with God are all great sources of blessing to consider. Where else are you experiencing blessings in your parenting?

CHALLENGE: CELEBRATE THIS! Plan a family celebration for what is going well in your home. Allow everyone in the house to participate. It can be a pizza dinner, a miniature golf outing, a night on the town, or a family game night. Make it better than a typical evening at home; try to exclude screen time so conversation can happen. Let the whole family know that the purpose of this event is to celebrate your family, parenting, cooperation, and the way you all connect to make your house a home.

There is nothing more important than parents passing on a generational legacy of faith and values to their children.

—*James Dobson*

14

Parenting Balance

JUST BECAUSE YOU were able to conceive, adopt, or foster a child, you are now expected to be a leader, a nurturing soul with rock-solid boundaries. You may even believe you have the ability to prepare your child for everything he will ever face or that you're a failure if something goes wrong.

Earlier I told you about my own labor story. My friend Meredith had a very different experience. In her pre-labor planning, we agreed that she would drop off her two older children at our house once labor was in full swing. Despite her excellent planning, she called to tell me to meet her at the hospital instead of dropping the kids off. Her third child arrived so quickly that the ER team met her at the door and made it less than 100 steps before stopping to deliver her little guy. Thankfully, her husband had gotten the car parked quickly so he could be there to witness the last moments of the event.

Not every labor is textbook; that's why we go to the hospital. Labor is a big deal, and sometimes we take it for granted. Living in a first-world country has given many of us a false sense that everything will be okay with every delivery. Sadly, that's not always true. I have held the hands of mothers and fathers and cried with family members when tiny babies have stayed in the hospital for months on end. I have been there when labor didn't end in life. And I have been there when a child's heart could not support the tiny body surrounding it.

As parents, there are heartbreaking moments that don't follow our pre-planned script and incredible events when help arrives just in time. There is no reason to believe you will parent without surprising moments. Every family will experience the unexpected from time to time, and there is no way to plan for some situations. But on the other hand, there are times where planning is exactly the best measure to aid in a situation.

The measure of successful living is balance. In business terms, when the balance is measured, it determines if improvement and change are causing new problems inside of the system. Let's apply that to parenting. When you make a change in one area, do you encounter off-balance experiences in other areas? If one child adds football practice, does that disrupt family mealtime? The key to bringing harmonious balance back into play is prioritization.

When you find yourself out of balance, take time with your spouse, partner, support system, mentor, or therapist to reconsider your priorities. Find someone to help you as a voice of reason—and take that wisdom for all it is worth.

Just a few weeks ago, I spoke with a woman who was in financial trouble. She had enrolled all of her four children in youth sports and quit her job to juggle the schedules. I can't help but think that her support system was not helping to provide the assistance she needed, nor was she seeking wise counsel. Irrational thinking is not a sign of balance, and I invite you to include people in your inner circle who can speak to you honestly when you are not thinking in *balance* terminology.

Have you ever attended a circus? The juggler begins by tossing two balls or handkerchiefs. Anybody can do that. Soon he adds bowling pins, hammers, plates, cups, eggs, or other precarious items. If you've ever noticed, the items he adds are to show off his skill—the more unbalanced, the better. Imagine what happens when he lets go of an egg and grabs a hammer. His muscles must be so skilled that he knows how to change the pressure and force being used to perform the trick. Not everyone can juggle, and we are astounded by people who are really good at it.

In your parenting world, you have a lot to juggle. If you find that you're dropping the ball, losing your balance, or focusing on the wrong part of the process, it is time to evaluate your juggling skills. Nobody carries the same load as anyone else. Pressure from other places in life may dictate how much you can manage in your parenting juggle, and you don't have to apologize when you simplify the process.

Start by taking out the big things, the ones that are obviously hard to control, and don't put them back until you are positive you can handle their impact. Even the best juggler doesn't juggle a clown or an elephant; he knows it will never work. The juggler knows that his capacity is limited, so he doesn't overload it.

Speaking of capacity and load, my favorite analogy for balance is a train. Each train car has a designated capacity. It can remain on the track only if it carries a load that is inside its limit. As more train cars are added, more engines will be needed to drive the train. Do you see where I'm going with this? The bigger the train you intend to pull with your own priorities, the bigger your support system must be.

It is the conductor's job to ensure the train is safe, and it's the job of the engineer to drive the train. The conductor is the leader of the crew and ensures that everyone knows and follows the rules. It is the engineer's job to make sure the cargo safely reaches its destination. See that partnership—parenting with a partner is just like this. Each of you needs to consider essential factors and help ensure balance is being maintained. If you plan to add more load, both the conductor and the engineer need to be aware and should work together to ensure the train will travel correctly. The engineer must stay on the right track, but the conductor ensures the train is operating correctly as it moves.

A train that is at total capacity with its load balanced correctly is in perfect rhythm. The click-clack noise on the track is a reminder of the rhythm that is being achieved. The efficiency of moving forward, carrying the maximum freight, and delivering it successfully is a magnificent feat. The rhythm in your family includes your schedule, family time, expectations, and values. When everything is prioritized correctly, the conductor can signal the engineer to move the train forward. This doesn't happen by accident, and the process is carefully managed.

Whether you are the conductor or the engineer is not for me to determine. Which role suits you best? The conductor arrives early, checks for safety, and considers risks. The engineer ensures movement, direction, and successful transit. Consider which adult fits each of these roles, or whether there is a bit of job sharing in your home. If you are a single parent, who can help you watch for pitfalls in the track or things that might derail your forward momentum?

You are not a train crew, but you are a team that must operate together to bring balance to the load of your shared responsibility. You must consider your capacity limitations and the load you are carrying. Success is your goal, and it is visually measured in balance. With that in mind, consider these questions:

- How do you share tasks?
- How do you support one another?
- What problems keep you from being in sync?
- How do you communicate when one member of the crew is not contributing correctly?
- Is your load bigger than your capacity?
- Is your train headed in the right direction?
- Do you need another locomotive pushing from behind? Do you need an enlarged support system?
- Is communication at its peak performance? If not, what should be adjusted?

There are many ways to parent, and there are many ways to contribute to the partnership of raising children. Your own parenting experience or your partner's experiences mixed with intention and values may come out in this conversation. This is a great time to set some goals and consider what balance-driven measures need to be invited into your home.

15

Structurally Sound Parenting

HAVE YOU EVER gone on a house hunt? It doesn't matter if you are renting or buying when you look for a house. What are the things that really matter? We bought a house in San Antonio, Texas, and our realtor worked really hard to listen to our wants and needs and fit them into our budget. Sure, we wanted a beautifully landscaped yard and a great location, but she wanted to ensure we had a solid foundation, sturdy walls, and a roof that would hold up in Texas rain. Her wisdom was essential in our house hunt, and the home inspector was the voice of reason as we looked at more than one home that turned out to be more work than we were able to afford.

We learned to listen to experts, to appreciate their wisdom, and to take their words very seriously. It would have been unwise to buy a home that we couldn't afford or one that would drain our savings with repairs. We had some construction experience, but we needed experts to stop us from moving in the wrong direction. People who want to sell their old home can cover up a lot of damage with cosmetic changes, but that doesn't really fix the issues. When it comes to having a great home, you don't just want a façade of a beautiful building; you want a well-constructed and well-maintained dwelling.

In the online assessment you took, the acronym STYLE defines how your family unit is influenced and how past influences have brought you to this juncture. Like the structure of a house, each section of the acronym builds the boundaries of your home. Let's take a closer look:

S - Stability
T - Tangible Experience
Y - Yourself
L - Lifestyle
E - Expectations

Stability

A few years ago, our family purchased an older home that needed to be remodeled. We were careful to look for things such as a solid foundation, a non-leaky roof, structurally sound walls, efficient appliances, newer HVAC and water heater, and highly rated insulation in the house-hunting process. The value of our home depended on these features, and we were hyper-aware of them with the multiple homes we visited. In the end, we chose a house that needed some remodeling, but the structure itself was very sound.

At the same time, we had friends who moved into a brand new home in Florida, and within a year, they noticed cracks in corners and a porch that began to sag. Underneath their home was a sinkhole that needed dozens of trucks full of concrete to fix. An old or new home can

Structurally Sound Parenting

be structurally sound, and either one can appear to look good on the surface but show signs of serious trouble. The foundation of a home is nothing to mess with, and the foundation of a family is just as critical.

Stability comes from the bottom and supports the entire structure. The base, the foundation, is the most critical part of the home and must be established before anything else. When a family begins without a great structure in place, additional support must be added to address the situation. It's not too late to add support under your foundation if it wasn't laid right in the first place; however, finding the proper support is important. A family therapist may be an essential part of that process.

Stability comes from your own family experience. The foundation you were exposed to as a child is often replicated in your own family structure. Whether formal or informal, your educational background helps to prepare you for future challenges that might arise. Your moral expectations and the spiritual footing of your home all come together to help you create a stable environment for your family.

Remember that you are blending your family with someone else if you are in a marriage or significant relationship. Your partner's family foundation, education, morals and values, upbringing, experience, and spiritual footing are just as necessary to evaluate, and any differences should optimally be ironed out before you start a family together.

We spoke earlier about the need for God to be an integral part of your parenting, and this is where that spiritual conversation is most critical. If you and your significant other are not on the same spiritual wavelength, there will be challenges ahead. It's a good idea to level the playing field before children enter the equation. If that's not possible, it's time to find that solid ground sooner rather than later. A pastor can help you with this conversation if you ask. This is not an area where your convictions should be overlooked.

Tangible Experience

Tangible things can be touched or experienced. It's much easier to have empathy when you understand something first hand. You are able to become introspective about an experience if you understand it fully. Parenting is an area where being introspective can help you determine if you are moving forward appropriately. It allows you to be action-oriented. If you discover repetitive patterns in your life, you might need help in solving problems, and you might be able to identify them in your family if you have had prior experience.

COVID has redefined the world you live in. The way you empathize with others has changed, and you have likely discovered a new level of exhaustion that you didn't think was possible. Additionally, parents have to be home more, cook more often, and socially distance themselves. Your tangible experiences have grown. Everyone has responded to the pandemic differently, and those experiences will influence the entire world for years to come.

Structurally Sound Parenting

The tangible experiences that influence your Parenting STYLE should help you become more determined to parent well. Your own painful experiences and their results in your life will dictate some of your parenting decisions. Your personal connections, attitude, growth experiences, determination, and memories all add up to create incredibly powerful boundaries in your relationships. You will allow these to seep into your decision-making, and modeling these tangible skills will develop your children's sense of ownership and life skills based on these tangible experiences.

If you have become overly confident, fearful, or pessimistic, your children will learn those attitudes and behaviors from you. If you have become merciful, kind, compassionate, and caring, you will pass those along as well. If you value joy, patience, understanding, communication, or spiritual matters, your kids will draw from your experiences to create behaviors either for or against your decisions.

Your positive experiences will typically draw your kids toward those same experiences, and your negative experiences will often repel your kids as they grow and begin making their own decisions. If you don't like something, your kids will often follow suit. If you didn't eat your vegetables, your kids may not either. But don't be surprised when they challenge the decisions you are making. They will have experiences that drive their adult years as well. Your job is to help shape their expectations so they are solid and dependable. The way you help your children to be well-rounded is by providing extensive experiences for them to form those opinions.

Yourself

It should come as no surprise that the person you are develops the structure of your family. Your emotional skills or lack of dynamic tools will shape the way your kids manage their own emotions. Your social experiences and how you handle social cues will influence how your kids operate in social settings. Awkwardness, self-esteem, confidence, hygiene, awareness of boundaries, and selfishness are highly affected by the way you carry yourself in the family unit. The way you model personal involvement, over-communication, under-communication, timeliness, fear, joy, and love will enable every member of your family to respond as you have.

Relational aptitude is the measurement of how you respond in relationships. It can also be explained through the EQ or emotional quotient. This is your ability to understand emotional connections or disconnections. You can use the feelings you have, whether physical or emotional, and manage yourself as you deal with stressful situations through communication and conflict resolution. It is important to practice offering grace and empathy to others. How well you operate in relationships matters, and passing this on to your kids does, too.

You have limitations, and learning to acknowledge them is part of this structural unit as well. You may be limited by education, resources, awareness, physical ability, disability, or even geography. Awareness is the key to success when it comes to limitations, the first step is to assess the limitation and then decide how much you can control its impact. Let go of the things you cannot control and take charge when you can.

Just like in the other categories of STYLE, I encourage you to consider how blending this aspect applies to others in your support system. If you are in a marriage, your limitations may be the same, but many of them will be unique to you as a person. How do you keep your limitations to a minimum? And what limitations can't be eliminated at all? Is there anything that has previously limited you that is no longer a threat?

Lifestyle

Lifestyle is the next section of our structure. Your lifestyle doesn't have to be lavish to have joy, harmony, peace, or even fun. Having a family doesn't have to be limited by your resources, but having kids is not free, either.

What does your lifestyle look like? Are you living inside your financial means? What image do you want your family to portray? Does your lifestyle measure up to the resources you have? Financial overextension is very real for some families, and overreaching the bounds of bank accounts can be dangerous. Do you find yourself falling into the temptation of looking at others who have been around for many years and have earned the things they have, but you want them now?

Managing expectations is the crucial role of this part of the structure. Do your kids know how to take care of what they have? Do they know how to handle the situation when you say "no" to their requests? Do you model good money management techniques? Have you helped them to understand value, the use of resources, and the meaning of wealth?

Joel was a dad who wanted a motorcycle, a boat, a beach house, and nearly every gadget available for his computer. His wife discovered their financial mess the day Joel's sports car was repossessed. His fourteen-year-old daughter was angry that her phone cord was inside the car when the bank removed it from their property. Joel's obsession with things had translated into selfish living and unrealistic expectations for his daughter. He realized the problems he had created, and today Joel is a financial planner who helps families to get their spending under control. His daughter works in his office and helps families teach their kids about money, too.

Andrea gave up her job when her baby was born. As a single mom, she lives in government housing and works hard to be a great mom. She recently revealed her resentful feelings about not owning a car. She felt trapped and without freedom. I asked her if she would be interested in getting a job to help increase her resources, and she said yes. She realized she had put herself into a limited lifestyle by staying home and not realizing what she was giving up when she stopped working toward the lifestyle she wanted. She and I talked about the value of freedom and how that needed to be balanced with being a mom. It doesn't have to be one or the other.

Your finances, stuff, gadgets, vehicles, social status, and well-being are all a part of your lifestyle. How does that influence your kids? How are you helping to manage their expectations? What does your wealth or lack of it dictate for your family? How can you value positive attitudes toward those whose lifestyle is not like yours?

Expectations

You have very personal expectations. You have made judgments of others and yourself that guide many of your thoughts and ideas. Your expectations define the experiences you will allow for yourself and your family.

Have you ever met someone who always expects to be right? He moves about the world thinking he knows it all and that you don't. Just how is it that he knows everything? His expectations have created limitations in his mind, and he expects everyone to listen to him, agree with him, and to follow his lead. He can't be reasoned with, either. Your opinions, ideas, and goals are not more or less important than those of others. To operate well inside societal norms, you need to learn to manage your expectations and teach your children the same skills.

Discernment happens when you weigh a decision or set of options and make a decision. When selfishness is the driving force, it will grow after the decision is made. The driving force is appropriately positioned when caring for others and considering needs over wants. It provides a measurement for discernment and making the right decisions. Consider the end result you want for yourself and for your family, and you will see just how vital your expectations are or how limited they should be. A great rule of thumb is to consider every person affected before making a decision.

Morals and values should also shape your decisions, and emotional decision-making should be limited. Buying a handbag outside of your budget because you want it is selfish. Buying it because the person selling it needs the money may not be the right reason either—but then again, it might. Buying the bag when you can afford it and when the purchase will not limit options for other family members is much more logical. You have an inner compass and tools, such as common sense and logic, to make decisions. The choice is yours to make, but note how self-centered you are in the process.

While parenting requires you to guide your kids, selfishness and demanding expectations should never be nurtured. A pastor friend once explained to me that all sin is selfishness. Consider that. Test it. I couldn't find a flaw in the statement. It has helped my perspective of selfish endeavors and has given me a simple way to discern the wisdom in decision-making. My kids can all quote the statement, and as they were growing up, I often asked them to consider their wishes based on that rule. It has made a massive difference in their expectations, too.

Earlier in the book, we discussed that the family compass—making intentionally direct, strategic, well-partnered parenting decisions together—is key.

Consider your own expectations, wants, and needs and weigh them evenly with those of your entire family. Be willing to bend and give or adjust as needed. Your kids need to see you model those skills. And they need to see you model the struggle to make the right choices. They will face similar challenges, and your example will prepare them as they determine balance and structure in their own adult journey.

What Matters Most?

Your opinions, your family, and your goals—these are all important, but they don't trump those of others. Your family structure must fit into a society that operates together. If you can envision your family unit as a house with four walls, a roof, and a solid foundation, you can visualize what matters most. Every family around you has its own structure. Some are more sound than others, and some have big houses while others have tiny apartments. Your home doesn't need to be a mansion; it needs to have great structure. Before comparing your family dynamic to someone else, consider how solidly and wisely you have constructed your family unit.

Four questions can help you with this assessment:

- What matters most in our home?
- What's best for our family today?
- What will cause adverse outcomes?
- What is the end goal that we are working toward?

Without defining success, you can never find it. Without knowing the goals you want to reach, you can never reach them. Without establishing a family unit, you can't be successful as a family. Without a successful family plan, you can't be a successful family leader. Your kids deserve the absolute best of your time, attention, and leadership.

How is your family STYLE structure setting up the next generation for success? Your decisions matter, and your example will influence the next generation and the one after it as well.

It is well known that we fear what we can't control, and we try to control what we fear. Are there fears in your parenting that are controlling the outcome of your work? What would have to happen for you to launch your kids into adulthood knowing that you have done your best and are confident that you have prepared them for success?

16

Phases of Parenting Power

MUCH OF WHAT you do in parenting is a result of your power to persuade. Any toddler in the toy aisle can show your power of persuasion to the public. The way you choose the battles you will fight is determined by the battles you are determined to win. How often must you be right? How much emphasis do you place on winning an argument? How important is it for your child to learn a lesson in the exact moment? Do you have what it takes to persuade your child to make the right choices, to follow the rules, or to obey?

In the phase in which your children are discovering how they express themselves, you have the ability to influence their words, their responses, and how they value your approval. And before you know it, they will change the way they respond. In time, a new phase will begin, and you have to figure it out all over again.

We have two identical wagons in our backyard. This week, we moved remnants of a large oak tree into our woodpile. We moved logs from one wagon into another and transferred the weight as we moved them uphill to their destination. We have another wagon that holds nearly a thousand pounds, but even though it can carry that much, it is often fruitless to weigh it down because it can't be moved by human strength. Using the three wagons, we worked to move the entire load. There were times we had to stop rolling and shift the weight. One wagon had less air in its tires and couldn't carry the same weight as its counterpart. The enormous tree took hours to cut up and move. We offloaded hundreds of pounds from one wagon to another. When the second wagon was ready, we filled it to capacity, and eventually, it was able to lift almost an entire load from the heavy-duty wagon. We were intentional about weight and were careful not to load both wagons to overflowing, because we knew we might have to take some of that weight back off. Working together and balancing the loads required all of the wagons, and the effort was beneficial.

We can't end this book without acknowledging the phase of adulthood. There are multiple changes that occur as you address your kids as adults, but they still ask for guidance in many cases. There are new rules for your relationships, and even if they still live at home, they are no longer children. Their attitudes and behaviors have different weights, and their responsibility has reached monumental levels. In this zone, they must live into their adulthood, and you must take your foot off the gas pedal and your hands off the steering wheel.

This stage is difficult because you may be paying some of the bills, and they may be making terrible choices. Go back to that balance conversation and look for the areas in which your load and capacity are no longer in alignment. Knowing you have prepared your kids for change and that you have laid out expectations, you have decisions to make that can alter their lives and yours, but they are no longer about behavior, shaping their values, or defining their obedience. In this stage, they need support, encouragement, and a lot of silence. When they make a mistake, they need to have the opportunity to ask for your guidance and support.

Just as with younger kids, they need to feel the weight of their actions. You will not agree with every decision they make, and they will not always make their decisions exactly as you would. In this time, they need your emotional and relational support, even if their actions say otherwise. Your solid footing, the way you model strength, and the tools you have equipped them with will come together as they discover the shape and style of their own adult journey. The foundation—Stability, Tangible experience, Yourself/themselves, Lifestyle choices, and Expectations—form together as they begin to plan for their own parenting journey.

As you slide into the mentor/coach role and leave the parenting role, you will see the blessings of your work; you can stop doing much of what you once felt responsible for and start encouraging your kids to make great choices that will influence others. You will have a front-row seat as you discover what is missing, what has been successful, where they have gotten hung up, and what communication is needed to help them—when they ask for it, of course.

You may now experience becoming a grandparent, bringing new members into the family, and modeling collaborative relationships. Your children will add to their own families in time, and your job will once again shift.

Finding your place in this experience is just as uncertain as every parenting phase. Still, openness, honesty, and communication are the critical components for finding the right amount of involvement.

Just like you stopped packing their lunches and washing their laundry, it is time for them to make discoveries on their own and for you to step back and allow them the freedom to grow. They might not look back or say thanks this time, but they will know you are their inspiration. Your choices have been intentional, and your influence is significant as they move into their own adult journey.

Not all parents will see their kids into adulthood at the same rate. Parenting a child with a disability, an emotional or attachment disorder, depression, anxiety, or another challenge may mean this journey is extended for your family. Patience, wisdom, and prayer are the keys to walking this pathway. Having a great support system will allow you to transition your parenting role into the support role with appropriate boundaries and expectations.

As you process this change in your children's lives, here are a few questions to ask:

- What do I want them to know?
- Who should be influencing their lives that will challenge them to grow?
- How can I facilitate their success?
- How will I define a win in this chapter of their lives?

Phases of Parenting Power

- Who will I celebrate with? How?
- How will I ask their permission to be involved in their decisions?
- What resources should I stop providing for them?
- What new or different expectations should I have?
- How will I support their spiritual lifestyle?
- What expectations are realistic?
- What rules should remain in our home, even though our kids are grown?

The most powerful way to change the world is to live in the front of our children the way we would like the world to be.

—*Graham R. White*

17

Parenting Leaders

IN THE QUEST to become the very best parent you can be, you must make some intentional investments. There's not just one school of thought on parenting success, and many parenting theories support your ideals while others contradict them. Your job is to raise your kids and somehow find balance and happiness in your own life. Pressures from work, extended family, financial obstacles, home repairs, cultural differences, politics, and religious beliefs can be mind-boggling. Add to that the various roles you play, which never seem to stop growing—that is a lot to juggle.

I have kept up with many parenting theorists throughout the years as they presented ideas on bonding, discipline, and simply showing up. It's a daunting task to wade through all of the good ideas that sit on the shelves of bookstores, right next to the bad.

As a parenting specialist, I have met with thousands of families, and I can't help but observe them everywhere I go. Some parents are much more invested than others, and some are much more successful. There is no direct correlation between any specific set of data and the better parent; there's no recipe to ensure your parenting STYLE or your tactics will help your children cross the finish line with ease. But there are some theoretical foundations worth considering.

Consider yourself in the driver's seat; you need to travel to a specific location. You're not going to take the long route, the windy route, or the bumpy route on purpose. During the entire trip, you are focused on the finish line, but sometimes potholes, detours, heavy traffic, and accidents derail your finest plans. Parenting theorist Reggie Joiner would urge you to "keep the end in mind." Don't change your final destination simply because you ran into a little trouble. This requires intentionality and changing your vehicle in each new phase of parenting you encounter.

I would add that the finish line is not birthday number eighteen. Your end goal is helping your child cross the finish line successfully—all the way until life is over. How are your decisions today equipping your child for his eightieth birthday? How about his ninetieth? How will your child manage life when a crisis emerges, when his education has short-changed him, or when his relationships are struggling?

Kristin Ivy's research has provided a glimpse into each phase of parenting. Children before age five think differently than they do in elementary, middle school, and high school. Because they move from artist to scientist, mathematician, problem solver, and philosopher as they age, your parenting needs to change with them. Remember our conversation about balance? Finding new balance, the right partnerships, and new motivational tools around your children are critical. The influences you approve for your children at each stage have louder voices than you do, and it is vital that you can trust the support system being built around them.

Dr. Kevin Lehman's parenting philosophy includes an understanding of the birth order your children fall into. Responsibility, compassion, stubbornness, independence, and defiance fall into interestingly predictable areas simply because of who was born first. Lehman adds to his parenting theory that you are in the driver's seat, and your own behaviors need to get fixed if you want to change your children's behaviors.

Kurt Bruner's influence on parenting is presented in his three-step theory: Be Jesus, show them Jesus, and raise them to be Christians. Kurt is passionate about fathers investing in their kids' lives and parents partnering with one another and the church to follow their family compass. He is a firm believer that broken families can find hope and healing.

Paul David Tripp's parenting theories are heart-centered. His philosophy of respect for authority requires parents to model respect for their kids. Tripp encourages parents to plan for change in long increments and not expect change to happen overnight.

Dave Stone's parenting philosophy centers around family time, investment, and intentional decisions. Helping kids to trust you requires you to support them, even when it is hard. Planning family time into your schedule requires commitment, and dinner time is an excellent opening for consistent and open communication.

I would encourage you to look into other parenting resources, to share them with your friends, and to look for the latest works of these great authors. Keep up with current research, weigh the bad and the good, and consider what really matters in each of their theories.

18

Introspective Parenting

INTROSPECTIVE PARENTING IS a different perspective from what you may be used to. Most parenting books tell you what you are doing right, how to stop doing it all wrong, or why your kids are special. Few books ask you to pause, have necessary conversations, and deeply think about how your past is influencing your future. The purpose of this book is for you to contemplate what matters most. I'd like to end with a few thoughts.

Like the end of a good movie, you can walk away and let this book simply rest in the arena of entertainment. You can turn to your friends and say something meaningful, or you could wipe your tears and hope nobody is looking. Regardless, you have responded to what you have been reading, and I would like to challenge you to sit with it for a bit. Don't just close the back cover and know you have had some great coffee conversations, but really let it sink in. Why do you parent the way you do? Is there a better way to do it? If so, what does that look like? What needs to change, and how soon?

For some of you, more commitment should be added to your parenting future: better communication, more partnership with your spouse, or helping one another out. For others, you have discovered actions you need to stop doing, habits you need to change, or investments you need to make.

Nobody is standing over your shoulder, requiring you to be a better parent. So why would you care in the first place? The answer is simple: because your children's lives depend on you. Their education, health, spiritual guidance, knowledge, understanding, mercy, kindness, goodness, and patience do, too. Their tenacity, their character, and even their haircuts will be influenced by you. The way they respond to others, to negativity, and to wonderful experiences will be a reflection of what they have seen in you.

As much as you stand up for your kids, you will begin to see that your role as a parent is not about helping them to be happy all the time. It's not about making their lives easier or giving them everything they want. Among the many tasks you carry out, first and foremost, you are a parent, and the life you have been entrusted with will be influenced by your faith, your actions, your words, and your investment.

You are a role model, a lobbyist, a nutritionist, and a historian. You are a teacher, a preacher, and a salesman, all in the same body. You must negotiate, train, and nurture. You must discern and bring wisdom to every situation. To do any of these, you must observe what is going on, consider what needs to change, and strategize how you will go about it. Your parenting style will lead you to act on all of this, and your ability to follow through will bring those actions into the spotlight. More than

Introspective Parenting

anything, you must be consistent and carefully consider each opportunity that lies ahead.

You may not be perfect like a unicorn or repulsive like a roach, but your parenting can be measured somewhere on that scale. You may wonder where you fall, and your family likely, already knows the answer. One thing is certain: your kids are grateful that you are asking, even if they don't know it. Their future friends, roommates, bosses, and spouses will thank you for investing. One day your kids may stop to thank you, though it's not likely unless they have had their own children who show appreciation. The point isn't a thank you note or a thumbs-up, though those moments are treasures. The point is that the next generation will be changed because you stepped up to be a better parent. A few generations down the road will likely have no idea that you made these choices, but your influence will still be around.

Section 2

Discovering Your Parenting STYLES

You are unique and have a combination of STYLEs. Consider which of these best fits who you are now:

- Your TRUE STYLE—The true you, even when nobody is around.
- Your REVERTED STYLE—The parts of parenting you don't have to work at.
- Your AVOIDANT STYLE—What you fear doing.
- Your HEALTHY STYLE—When you're living here, you know it, and it's good.

Take the online assessment to discover more about your top STYLEs.

The Ant Parent

> **Quotable Quote:**
>
> Study while others are sleeping; work while others are loafing; prepare while others are playing, and dream while others are wishing.
>
> —William A. Ward

In Nature: A group of ants is called a colony.

Ants work together. Inside the colony everyone has a role and a set of expectations. Teamwork is their mantra. Ants work on big and small projects, and they work for the greater good.

As a parent, your *Ant* STYLE stands out because:

You know there is an extensive list of tasks to be done, and you expect everyone at your house to do his or her part. You are initiative-driven and see the value of a group effort. You work hard at parenting and expect your kids to work hard at growing up. You model reasonable expectations for your kids.

Words you might connect with:

Excellence, initiative, growth, together, and finished.

A snapshot of the household influenced by the *Ant* parent:

Your kids know how to work hard and work together because you have modeled that for them.

As a parenting partner:

As an Ant parent, you equate love with tasks, achievement, and emotional satisfaction. Your partner must understand the drive to complete tasks and the desire to teach your kids to get along with each other. You need a hard-working partner who shares the parenting role equally.

Others will know they have spotted the *Ant* parenting STYLE when:

Family meetings and chore charts are key indicators that you have met an Ant parent. The kids are seen behind the cash register or cleaning the stockrooms of the family business. The children help with housework and chores, and family members work together to achieve various goals. This parent may seem to have unending energy.

The Ant Parent

Pros and cons of the *Ant* parenting STYLE:

Pros: Your kids are team players and understand that there are various roles on the team. Your family members celebrate joy when goals are met. You help your kids see the value of seeing a project through to the end. You model hard work and innovation, wise investment of time, and group affirmation.

Cons: Your kids grow up expecting their peers to work hard and may be disappointed or let down by lazy people. They may be resentful of the high expectations required by authority figures. You may observe your kids becoming over-achievers or significant under-achievers. You may become too focused on the goal and miss the journey.

Scriptures based on the assessment results:

"Share their burdens, and so complete Christ's law" (Galatians 6:2).

"And mark that you do this with humility and discipline—not in fits and starts, but steadily, pouring yourselves out for each other in acts of love" (Ephesians 4:2).

Introspective thinking:

Use this section to consider the questions and thoughts that you connect with. How can you become a better parent by considering what should be done differently? How should you actively celebrate your current successes? How should you strategize ways to connect with your children and family more intentionally? What are your parenting priorities? My task list includes:

- Teamwork, helping others, dreaming big, and caring about others—not just for my family. What expectations do I have that are too big for my team?
- I thrive in low drama and high production environments. Does my family know that?
- Am I introverted or extroverted? Do I balance other people's needs and their tasks with my own?
- Do I prioritize the needs of others over my own needs?
- I am a problem solver; how can I pass that on to my kids?
- When there is chaos, I look for a solid strategy. In what ways am I teaching my children the skills of strategic thinking?
- It is so important to teach my kids to lead and to follow. There is a time for each.
- Are my kids trying to be like me? Have I asked them how I can be a better leader to my family?
- Are my kids team players even when I'm not the one giving directions? How can I encourage them?
- What is the most significant step I need to take to be a better parent? How will I know that I have succeeded?

The Bear Parent

> **Quotable Quote:**
>
> All of us parents and grandparents suffer this disease—of expecting our child to be someone extraordinarily fantastic.
>
> —Sunita Rajwade

In Nature: A group of bears is called a sleuth.

Bears are territorial, and their area can be huge. Bear parents lead, and their cubs must stay close behind. Bear parents are teachers and protectors with high expectations for cubs to learn to catch fish and protect the family. Bear moms have been known to give birth in their sleep. Now that's a serious nap!

As a parent, your *Bear* STYLE stands out because:

You are in charge; there's no doubt about that. Your children should listen, watch, and learn from you. You have so much knowledge to instill in them. You are a great teacher, have high expectations, and above all, you are a protector. You see things clearly and want your kids to respond appropriately.

Words you might connect with:

Obedience, consistency, authority, expectations, and strength.

A snapshot of the household influenced by the *Bear* parent:

Your kids know how to rise to a big challenge. Your expectations have shown them why.

As a parenting partner:

You partner well with a highly organized individual who is well scheduled and has high expectations. Anyone with a high-achieving, consistent parenting STYLE can be a great partner for you, but a laid-back partner may help balance your high-pressure tendencies.

The Bear Parent

Others will know they have spotted the *Bear* parenting STYLE when:

"No" means "no!" and the kids know it. Bear parents do not negotiate with their kids. Children look to their parents when a question is asked of the family. Kids always ask permission.

Pros and cons of the *Bear* parenting STYLE:

Pros: Your children respect that you are "in charge." You set boundaries and check them to ensure that they are not crossed. Your children know they can depend on your choices. You have children who are well behaved in public places. You expect your kids to be high achievers, and they often are.

Cons: Your children may fear failure and sometimes feel they lack room for personal expression. They may choose rebellious actions or misbehave. Your children may not have a connected relationship you, though they respect or fear you.

Scriptures based on the assessment results:

"Point your kids in the right direction—when they're old they won't be lost" (Proverbs 22:6).

"A good life gets passed on to the grandchildren; ill-gotten wealth ends up with good people" (Proverbs 13:22).

"At the time, discipline isn't much fun. It always feels like it's going against the grain. Later, of course, it pays off big-time, for it's the well-trained who find themselves mature in their relationship with God" (Hebrews 12:11).

Introspective thinking:

Use this section to consider the questions and thoughts that you connect with. How can you become a better parent by considering what should be done differently? How should you actively celebrate your current successes? How should you strategize ways to connect with your children and family more intentionally?

- When I consider the term "force of nature," does that better apply to my parenting or my child's behavior?
- Have I already made up my mind regarding the outcome before I ask my children questions or for their opinions?
- Is there room for my children to ask questions or openly ask for more instruction?
- On a scale of 1 to 10, how often do I make decisions and expect my children to follow my directions?
- How do I handle my parenting when someone else's ideals contradict my own?
- In what ways could I improve my relationship with my children?

- In what ways am I most proud of my children's achievements? Have I told them?
- Do I give my kids room to dream their own dreams? How do I shape those dreams?
- What words do I use to encourage my kids? How often do I use them?
- What is the most significant step I need to take to be a better parent? How will I know that I have succeeded?

The Clownfish Parent

Quotable Quote:

Parenting is the biggest sacrifice one can make. It's putting your life on hold to fulfill the promise of your children's tomorrows.

—Fredrica Ehimen

In Nature: A group of clownfish is called a school.

Clownfish live among anemone to protect themselves and their young from predators. They make a clearing for their eggs and fan them to aid in hatching. To be able to do this, they cover themselves in mucus so they won't be stung by the paralyzing tentacles of the anemone. The young survive because the parents make the water cloudy if they sense danger nearby.

As a parent, your *Clownfish* STYLE stands out because:

You know your kids are worth everything you have to give in time, money, or sacrifice. You will do almost anything to provide and protect them. Your kids are expected to give their best, and you have grace when they don't. You work hard to set your kids up to win. Sometimes you think this is your STYLE because it is what others expect from you.

Words you might connect with:

Protective, pragmatic, supportive, empathetic, and realistic.

A snapshot of the household influenced by the *Clownfish* parent:

Your kids know you will acknowledge their hard work and help them achieve their dreams.

As a parenting partner:

You need a partner who balances your grace-giving tendencies. You need a rule enforcer and a consistent parenting partner to ensure your kids are well-rounded and have realistic expectations in life. You must both communicate well to keep from being frustrated. Above all, you and your partner must stay united.

The Clownfish Parent

Others will know they have spotted the *Clownfish* parenting STYLE when:

The Clownfish parent is present and focused on the challenges ahead. For example, during parent-teacher conferences take in the whole picture and not just one aspect. Don't get lost in conversation, but pay close attention to what must be changed, adjusted, or removed to find success? Additionally, the parent may find extra tools to help his or her child succeed, even if it means working extra hours or taking on a part-time job.

Pros and cons of the *Clownfish* parenting STYLE:

Pros: Your kids know they are loved. You have given them what they need to achieve your hopes and dreams. You expect your kids to achieve great things, and they thrive in the spotlight.

Cons: Others won't sacrifice for you in the real world, so your kids might have to work hard to win or even be in the running. Your kids may fear letting you down when they can't achieve what you expect of them. They may be over-achievers or they may rebel through underachievement. You may try to live vicariously through your children's dreams.

Scriptures based on the assessment results:

"Friends, don't complain about each other. A far greater complaint could be lodged against you, you know. The Judge is standing just around the corner" (James 5:9).

"And if some bullying Assyrian shows up, invades and violates our land, don't worry. We'll put him in his place, send him packing, and watch his every move" (Micah 5:6).

"God is there, ready to help; I'm fearless no matter what. Who or what can get to me?" (Hebrews 13:6).

Introspective thinking:

Use this section to consider the questions and thoughts that you connect with. How can you become a better parent by considering what should be done differently? How should you actively celebrate your current successes? How should you strategize ways to connect with your children and family more intentionally?

- Do I believe family is everything? Will I do everything for my family? How exhausting is this?
- As a Clownfish parent, I may say, "I work hard to provide for my kids' wants and whims, but I don't need much for myself." How do I take time for myself to re-energize? Is it enough? Why?
- What do I say about my children's future? Write down your thoughts, such as: "I work hard to provide, so my kids' hopes and dreams are met."
- I don't want my kids to miss out, so I will give up _____. Is there a limit? What is it?

- What other words would you use? As a Clownfish parent, I am highly protective, highly involved, highly sacrificial, and _____.
- Could you say: "My children don't realize how well they have it" or "My kids easily miss the value of the things I provide for them"? How can you help them to learn value?
- How do I help my kids learn gratitude, appreciation, and thankfulness? Am I intentional about helping them to understand these values?
- What concerns me most as a parent? Does it matter how others see our family or how my kids interact with the world around them?
- Do I ever feel burned out or resentful toward my family and friends? How can I improve that?
- What is the most significant step I need to take to be a better parent? How will I know that I have succeeded?

The Dolphin Parent

> **Quotable Quote:**
>
> To be in your children's memories tomorrow, you have to be in their lives today.
>
> —Barbara Johnson

In Nature: A group of dolphins is called a pod.

Looking for dolphins is a great pastime for boating tourists. Dolphins know how to steal the show in the wild and in aquariums. A dolphin will sleep deeply by turning off one part of its brain while paying attention to danger with the other part.

As a parent, your *Dolphin* STYLE stands out because:

You are the rudder of the ship. The rest of the world struggles to keep up with your family, and you find a way to fit it all in. You live for potential, optimism, and possibility. When it comes to others, you care and are thoughtful. You are the master of providing opportunities for others to grow. You want your kids to be considerate. Your calendar meticulously keeps your family in sync.

Words you might connect with:

Productive, encourager, fun, optimistic, and potential.

A snapshot of the household influenced by the *Dolphin* parent:

Your children know how to have an optimistic outlook on life. You see them as considerate, and they follow a schedule well.

As a parenting partner:

You need a partner who understands your need to be on the move. Top communication skills are required and will be expected from every member of your family for the sake of survival. Be sure you are listening to and spending time with your partner, not just the kids.

The Dolphin Parent

Others will know they have spotted the *Dolphin* parenting STYLE when:

Decked out in team gear, the Dolphin parent drives the family mobile and ensures his or her kids are on time (or close) everywhere they go. This parent has logistics down to a science and is cheering for every family member right after making just one more phone call.

Pros and cons of the *Dolphin* parenting STYLE:

Pros: Your kids are good at managing their time, or at least they know how to follow the leader who holds the calendar. Your kids can multi-task because they have learned to be efficient. They can do homework in the car between events and respond to change better than their peers. They juggle priorities such as school, work, sports, and vacations like pros. Finally, your kids are good at doing many tasks simultaneously, because they are exposed to lots of different things.

Cons: There is usually very little family time built into the Dolphin schedule. Be careful to plan for it and notice when your kids are tired or overwhelmed. Once you become an empty-nester, you may struggle to adapt in other relationships. There is a lot of pressure on every family member to achieve and perform. Dolphin parents, your kids don't set their own schedules or even know how, so be sure to teach those skills. Help your kids stay free from guilt when they underperform or express a lack of self-esteem when they are out of the spotlight.

Scriptures based on the assessment results:

"We humans keep brainstorming options and plans, but God's purpose prevails" (Proverbs 19:21).

"Write these commandments that I've given you today on your hearts. Get them inside of you and then get them inside your children. Talk about them wherever you are, sitting at home or walking in the street; talk about them from the time you get up in the morning to when you fall into bed at night" (Deuteronomy 6:6–7).

"Careful planning puts you ahead in the long run; hurry and scurry puts you further behind" (Proverbs 21:5).

Introspective thinking:

Use this section to consider the questions and thoughts that you connect with. How can you become a better parent by considering what should be done differently? How should you actively celebrate your current successes? How should you strategize ways to connect with your children and family more intentionally?

- Maximum experience and maximum organization equal maximum productivity. What expectations help me reach my maximum parenting potential?
- Organization keeps the entire system efficiently on track. How can I simplify the organization in my home?

- Everyone is a team player and needs to be on the same team. How do I parent when my kids don't feel like being team players?
- Highly socialized kids thrive in social settings. How can I help my kids gain in their social awareness?
- PTA parent, label-maker mom, or system-architect dad might be a title I aspire to earn. How do these titles help me to parent more effectively? How do they hinder me?
- Dolphin parents need a break, too. How do I take a break? How am I modeling rest and recharging habits for the kids?
- What's next? As each child enters a new phase, I have new milestones to approach: walking, talking, dancing, throwing, reading, driving, and others. How can I make the next milestone memorable?
- Just for a moment, I need to carefully and quietly consider my top three priorities. How do I keep myself well-grounded? How can I be sure the kids are on level ground as well?
- How often do I take time to find calm, quiet, and peace? Do I find comfort in this space?
- What is the most significant step I need to take to be a better parent? How will I know that I have succeeded?

The Eagle Parent

> **Quotable Quote:**
>
> You don't own your children. You can't control your children. They weren't given to you for those reasons. Love them. Show them. Encourage them. Help them strengthen their wings. Teach them to fly.
>
> —Author Unknown

In Nature: A group of eagles is called a convocation.

We are fascinated by how an eagle mother will swoop down and catch her young during flying lessons. Saving the day, she will catch her eaglet just before it hits the ground. Her majestic wings help her bring the young eagle back to the nest to help prepare it for adulthood. Huge nests on high cliffs are great for protection.

As a parent, your *Eagle* STYLE stands out because:

You are in your strongest parenting stance when your kids are pushing against boundaries or nearing danger. Your kids make mistakes, and you know it, so stop them and address them directly. You let your kids fail, but you stay involved to ensure they don't make a total mess of things. You operate as an invisible fence and help set boundaries. Much like a lifeguard, you are always watching for the need to step in, but you choose to let your capable kids figure out the best options to solve their problems.

Words you might connect with:

Awareness, problem solver, reliable, protective, and realistic.

A snapshot of the household influenced by the *Eagle* parent:

Your kids know you will be there when times get tough. They know they can talk to you about their problems and that you will provide wise guidance.

As a parenting partner:

The best partner for you is someone who understands your weaknesses and can balance them out. A calm-spirited, highly communicative parent can soften

The Eagle Parent

your approach and help your strengths shine. Your hyper-awareness of parenting challenges can help other parenting types to be successful.

Others will know they have spotted the *Eagle* parenting STYLE when:

Eagle parents allow their children to have freedom, though they are tethered to the source. They are watching from the sidelines and can fix any mess their children get into. They may exhibit less fear than other parents, but they work hard to keep the damage under control.

Pros and cons of the *Eagle* parenting STYLE:

Pros: As an Eagle parent, you are involved, and your kids know it. Your kids know they can depend on you for support. They have the freedom to make mistakes and learn from them. Your children know right from wrong on a deep level.

Cons: Your kids might not notice boundaries because they never actually get all the way to them. You might bail them out before lessons are fully learned. They might make the same mistakes in cycles. Your kids may avoid asking for help because of fear of micromanagement.

Scriptures based on the assessment results:

"But those who wait upon God get fresh strength. They spread their wings and soar like eagles, They run and don't get tired, they walk and don't lag behind" (Isaiah 40:31).

"If there are corrections to be made or manners to be learned, God can handle that without your help" (Romans 14:4).

"He must handle his own affairs well, attentive to his own children and having their respect" (1 Timothy 3:4).

Introspective thinking:

Use this section to consider the questions and thoughts that you connect with. How can you become a better parent by considering what should be done differently? How should you actively celebrate your current successes? How should you strategize ways to connect with your children and family more intentionally?

- As a parent, do I teach my kids that society builds the framework for protection? How do I instill the purpose of my role?
- How have I encouraged my kids to listen to my warnings? Do they know when I will step in to help?
- This thought resonates with me: "I said it once." How important is first-time obedience?
- My kids might not learn to save themselves from failure. What is my role when they enter unsafe or chaotic waters?
- Patience requires intention. In what specific ways can I grow in patience with my children?

The Eagle Parent

- At times, my kids need to be shown proper boundaries, and sometimes they need to push against those boundaries to test their ability to make wise decisions. How do I know the difference?
- If I could give my friends one piece of parenting advice, what would it be? Do they see me as a strong parent? Why?
- Sometimes kids are jealous of others. How do I coach my children when they are mistreated or when someone is jealous of their lifestyle?
- As my kids grow, so do their boundaries. What does this mean in our home? How does this define my role as a parent?
- What is the most significant step I need to take to be a better parent? How will I know that I have succeeded?

The Flamingo Parent

> **Quotable Quote:**
>
> Promise me you'll always remember:
> You're braver than you believe and stronger than you seem, and smarter than you think.
>
> —A. A. Milne

In Nature: A group of flamingos is called a flamboyance.

Flamingos are small families with a mother, a father, and just one chick. The adults mate when it is raining to ensure the flock will have provisions. The young are hatched in large numbers across the flock. They thrive in their small group, and the parents are devastated if the chick is injured or dies. Both parents care for their young, and both can produce milk. They have a special nutrient they feed the chick, so it too will turn pink. The parents can lose their color by providing for the young.

As a parent, your *Flamingo* STYLE stands out because:

You value tightly bonded relationships. You are most content when your family spends meaningful time together. Quality time, family game night, and commitment to tradition are as common as hugs and the abundance of affection in your home. As Flamingo parents, you truly love each other and outwardly express that. Tradition is important because it connects you to the past and guides your future.

Words you might connect with:

Purpose, initiative, nurture, life experience, and intention.

A snapshot of the household influenced by the *Flamingo* parent:

Your kids demonstrate affection and admiration for others because of your example. They find safety and well-being when others are friendly.

The Flamingo Parent

As a parenting partner:

You prefer to partner with an individual who possesses a broad support system. You want the children to be well-rounded, so you will expose them to many topics of discussion. You will need an adventurous partner with a high level of courage to bring purpose to the family unit.

Others will know they have spotted the *Flamingo* parenting STYLE when:

This parent is rubbing a child's back or nursing the baby. Flamingos are highly engaged and heavily involved. They will push the swings as long as needed. They may even ride down the slide. The toys they purchase are often educational. They often have a well-established community.

Pros and cons of the *Flamingo* parenting STYLE:

Pros: As Flamingos, you are typically a very close family. Your family members are there to support each other and to lend a hand when needed or stay strong in tough times. Your children's emotions matter. When in trouble, the kids tend to turn toward family members before friends.

Cons: Your kids demonstrate affection and admiration for others because of your example. They find safety and wellbeing when others are friendly.

Scriptures based on the assessment results:

"Be gentle with one another, sensitive. Forgive one another as quickly and thoroughly as God in Christ forgave you" (Ephesians 4:32).

"May God our Father himself and our Master Jesus clear the road to you! And may the Master pour on the love so it fills your lives and splashes over on everyone around you, just as it does from us to you. May you be infused with strength and purity, filled with confidence in the presence of God our Father when our Master Jesus arrives with all his followers" (1 Thessalonians 3:11–13).

"And regardless of what else you put on, wear love. It's your basic, all-purpose garment. Never be without it. Let the peace of Christ keep you in tune with each other, in step with each other. None of this going off and doing your own thing. And cultivate thankfulness" (Colossians 3:14–15).

Introspective thinking:

Use this section to consider the questions and thoughts that you connect with. How can you become a better parent by considering what should be done differently? How should you actively celebrate your current successes? How should you strategize ways to connect with your children and family more intentionally?

- Discipline includes love and hugs, direction, and firm conversation—corrections first, and

affirmation included. What other parenting thoughts do I have that are part of my core values?
- As a parent, am I aware of the need for my children to develop their own identities and not what I have chosen for them?
- How do I manage unexpected situations? What are my strengths and weaknesses?
- How do I clearly define goals and expectations so my children will be able to meet the goals?
- Who is in my circle of influence for advice and problem-solving? Who would I like to invite?
- Have I inserted a glass ceiling into my children's lives? If so, what should I do about it?
- Do I have a hard time letting go of the past or wrongdoing? Why does implementing discipline hurt me?
- Do I dance between logic and emotion? Do I find that urgent matters lobby for top priority in my parenting?
- When it comes to parenting, am I rational?
- What is the most significant step I need to take to be a better parent? How will I know that I have succeeded?

The Hawk Parent

> **Quotable Quote:**
>
> The solution to every parenting problem starts with nine little words: 'I'm here.' 'I hear you.' 'How can I help?' When needs are met through connection, hearts are opened to gentle, respectful, and compassionate correction.
>
> —L.R. Knost

In Nature: A group of hawks is called a kettle.

This parent takes "watch you like a hawk" to a whole new level. This saying came about because of the hawk's keen sense of sight. A hawk can see up to twenty miles away and can focus on two things simultaneously. "Hawk-eyed" means being vigilant, watchful, or observant. Hawks also can turn their eyes from telescopes to microscopes in flight to seek after tiny prey. But it is the hawk's almost-human qualities of anger, love, and playfulness that have made them the favorite of many bird lovers.

As a parent, your *Hawk* STYLE stands out because:

You are very aware of your children and their surroundings. You stay close to your kids, and you are there to protect them, guide them, and lead them toward the right path. You look for perfection in yourself and others and hope your kids exhibit the behaviors you desire. You are intentional with your calendar, and you model investing in the right areas of life. You make commitments based on the strengths of each child.

Words you might connect with:

Individuality, consistent, stable, provide, and practical.

A snapshot of the household influenced by the *Hawk* parent:

You have taught your kids how to please you and others, and they know how to rise to the expectations of others.

The Hawk Parent

As a parenting partner:

As a Hawk, you need a parenting partner who is patient and willing to allow room for your kids to fail. You need the home to be well-rounded, and you need to find ways to let the kids and other family members solve problems. It's important to let others make decisions, to delegate, and to let responsibilities be expectations with your partner and your kids.

Others will know they have spotted the *Hawk* parenting STYLE when:

The Hawk parent is aware of the wins and losses the children experience. Failure is not an option, and making sure the kids are safe and secure is essential. The Hawk parent is consistent, and the kids learn they can always depend on their parent's presence.

Pros and cons of the *Hawk* parenting STYLE:

Pros: Your kids understand the relationship between themselves and authority. Your family unit is closely knit. As a Hawk, your kids know that expectations will be given, and if they are not, they should ask.

Cons: Your kids may not be good at making hard decisions. They may not easily make friends with their peers. Your children may not know the background or context of problems and may have trouble sorting that out inside peer or relational issues.

Scriptures based on the assessment results:

"Give your entire attention to what God is doing right now, and don't get worked up about what may or may not happen tomorrow. God will help you deal with whatever hard things come up when the time comes" (Matthew 6:34).

"Consider it a sheer gift, friends, when tests and challenges come at you from all sides. You know that under pressure, your faith-life is forced into the open and shows its true colors. So don't try to get out of anything prematurely. Let it do its work so you become mature and well-developed, not deficient in any way" (James 1:2-4).

Introspective thinking:

Use this section to consider the questions and thoughts that you connect with. How can you become a better parent by considering what should be done differently? How should you actively celebrate your current successes? How should you strategize ways to connect with your children and family more intentionally?

- I love my kids so much that I want to be with them all of the time. How do I help my kids gain independence when I can't be around?
- Our family is closely knit. How can I help my children to make friends with others?

The Hawk Parent

- I love scouts, class parties, and dance competitions. I'm in the front row. How do I help my children succeed even when they are homebodies?
- My kids don't have to worry about making bad decisions; I'll be there to help them. How does this help them? How does it hinder their growth?
- I document every milestone, and I take a lot of pictures. How can I help my child learn that some memories stand above others?
- Our trophy shelf, t-shirt drawer, and ribbon wall are enormous. How can I help my child keep only a few mementos of their success?
- Things are collected to have memories. What stories are you helping your kids remember so they can pass them on to the next generation?
- Help! My kids won't move out of the house. I don't mind it, but when will they be independent?
- I take a deep sigh when I think of my children. I love them deeply. I hope they know I'll always be here for them. I want to be their friend. That's a good thing—right?
- What is the most significant step I need to take to be a better parent? How will I know that I have succeeded?

The Lion Parent

> **Quotable Quote:**
>
> You never know how strong you are until being strong is the only choice you have.
>
> —Bob Marley

In Nature: A group of lions is called a pride.

The lion teaches the cubs to hunt by helping them find their prey. If they succeed, they are rewarded. If a cub struggles to kill its prey, the lion will step in and weaken the prey, giving the cub another chance to succeed. If that still isn't enough, the lion steps in again, giving a boost, then she lets the cub try again.

As a parent, your *Lion* STYLE stands out because:

As a Lion parent, you know you are in charge, and you offer needed grace, mercy, love, and empathy to others at the moment. The big picture matters to you, and you don't get lost in the details. As your family grows, you have more grace to offer. Your kids ask lots of questions, and you like it that way. You love to see your kids play and live the lives they have been given. You are often on guard for the protection of your kids.

Words you might connect with:

Protective, playful, experiential, coach, and connectedness.

A snapshot of the household influenced by the *Lion* parent:

You have modeled empathy and kindness for your kids, and they understand the need for both within the bounds of daily living.

As a parenting partner:

You partner well with a confident parenting style. You communicate well when prompted, but you wait for your family to ask for help. Your supportive parenting stance can complement many parenting styles. You need to be taken seriously in the parenting partnership.

Others will know they have spotted the *Lion* parenting STYLE when:

Lion parents are protective teachers until their children no longer listen. They help the kids try and try again. They may get frustrated with the children and outwardly express that. Lion parents are always on guard.

Pros and cons of the *Lion* parenting STYLE:

Pros: As a Lion, you are very gracious with your kids when they are young and give them room to make mistakes, even though your expectations are high. Your kids know your home is a safe place to fail.

Cons: As a Lion parent, you may punish at times when your children don't expect it. You may need to be reminded to set expectations early. You may appear as a pushover, letting kids get away with too much. Your kids will often reason their way out of responsibility and much-needed redirection. If your childrean are unsuccessful at a task, you may say, "That's okay; try again later." Too much "trying again" may create lazy kids.

Scriptures based on the assessment results:

"Discipline your children; you'll be glad you did— they'll turn out delightful to live with (Proverbs 29:17).

"Don't you see that children are God's best gift? the fruit of the womb his generous legacy? Like a warrior's fistful of arrows are the children of a vigorous youth.

Oh, how blessed are you parents, with your quivers full of children! Your enemies don't stand a chance against you; you'll sweep them right off your doorstep" (Psalm 127:3–5)

"God-loyal people, living honest lives, make it much easier for their children" (Proverbs 20:7).

Introspective thinking:

Use this section to consider the questions and thoughts that you connect with. How can you become a better parent by considering what should be done differently? How should you actively celebrate your current successes? How should you strategize ways to connect with your children and family more intentionally?

- Some people see me as an actor or showman. Like some lions, do I act out what I wish my kids would follow? What am I acting out? What about my family?
- What is more important: for the house to be clean or for the kids to meet my high expectations?
- Am I overly grace-filled? Do I allow the kids to trade respect for grace as they get older? Am I the backbone of the family in transition? Do I take time to listen to their input?
- The Lion parent is good at breaking down difficult tasks into bite-sized objectives. Do I oversimplify tasks for my kids? Do I expect too little?

The Lion Parent

- If there are two parents in the home, the Lion parent is often the one the kids come to when they are struggling. Why?
- Legacy, virtue, and family pride are words that describe a Lion parent. What other words should I add?
- Should there be a limit to "Try, try, try again"?
- As my kids get older, they will understand their parents better. How do I want my kids to emulate me? Do I listen to them and include their input?
- Being playful is part of my parenting STYLE. How do I bring the fun into our home?
- What is the most significant step I need to take to be a better parent? How will I know that I have succeeded?

The Lizard Parent

> **Quotable Quote:**
>
> Parenting shouldn't feel like a competitive sport; it's plenty challenging without added obstacles. Strive to be loving and kind. Have the courage to ask for help. Take a break when you need it, celebrate all the great stuff, and be kind to yourself. Be yourself. That's who your kid loves anyways.
>
> —Ariadne Brill

In Nature: A group of lizards is called a lounge.

Lizards are not very affectionate with their young. In fact, they are known to leave their eggs in the wild right after they are laid, which is probably why they lay so many. Many lizards struggle to grow up and may struggle when presented with danger. Young lizards may work together to be stronger as they grow up.

As a parent, your *Lizard* STYLE stands out because:

You are fun, and you bring the party. You may not directly shape and develop your children as much as the collective village will. Teachers, caregivers, grandparents, and others greatly influence your children's lives, and you are okay with that. You know your kids will turn out well, and you don't have to be the person to ensure that happens. Your children's growing independence will be a direct result of your parenting.

Words you might connect with:

Permissive, fun, freedom, approval, and community.

A snapshot of the household influenced by the *Lizard* parent:

Your kids know you love them because your influence is strongest in the fun times.

As a parenting partner:

Your partner in parenting needs you to know how important your role is. You need a strong parenting partner who is consistent and willing to help your kids learn accountability. This partner can help you connect with your kids relationally. Be aware of the need to help balance out the demands in your home.

The Lizard Parent

Others will know they have spotted the *Lizard* parenting STYLE when:

You'll recognize a Lizard parent because the time with the kids (possibly only part of the time) will always be awesome. The kids will remember the Lizard as the best parent ever, though there may be competition with others (sometimes an ex or grandparents). Even if it means going into debt, the kids will know how terrific the parent is. A Lizard parent may use gifts or rewards strategically to influence the kids.

Pros and cons of the *Lizard* parenting STYLE:

Pros: Your kids learn to be independent and pave their own way. Your family members understand freedom and enjoy it.

Cons: Your kids know how to duck, pivot, and respond because you have given them opportunities to learn how to respond to unorthodox situations. They may learn these skills earlier than their peers.

Scriptures based on the assessment results:

"I'm telling you that anyone who is so much as angry with a brother or sister is guilty of murder. Carelessly call a brother 'idiot!' and you just might find yourself hauled into court. Thoughtlessly yell 'stupid!' at a sister and you are on the brink of hellfire. The simple moral fact is that words kill. This is how I want you to conduct yourself in these matters. If you enter your place of worship and, about to make an offering, you suddenly remember a grudge a friend has against you, abandon your offering, leave immediately, go to this friend and make things right. Then and only then, come back and work things out with God" (Matthew 5:22–24).

"Anyone who neglects to care for family members in need repudiates the faith. That's worse than refusing to believe in the first place" (1 Timothy 5:8).

"Don't be afraid to correct your young ones; a spanking won't kill them" (Proverbs 23:13).

Introspective thinking:

Use this section to consider the questions and thoughts that you connect with. How can you become a better parent by considering what should be done differently? How should you actively celebrate your current successes? How should you strategize ways to connect with your children and family more intentionally?

- How do I communicate with the nanny or grandma to ensure she takes good care of the kids?
- When I'm around, I'm in charge. Do my kids need me to show them who is in charge when I'm not around?
- My kids are going to have fun when I'm around. Is it possible to go overboard?

- I want great things for my kids, even if I have to work 100 hours a week to make it happen. Do you think they will want to be my friend when they grow up?
- I don't necessarily have great relationship skills in all areas of my life. Who can help my kids grow those skills or help me figure out the things I don't know or understand about my parenting?
- My life has sometimes been interrupted by people with toxic patterns. How do I make sure my kids see the truth in those patterns and don't get hurt as I have?
- When I contemplate my parenting, I am aware that my kids need parents, but I struggle to see how my parenting will shape them significantly. Should I work on this more?
- What are my priorities? How can I help others around me to instill those priorities in my children?
- Enjoying life means living in the moment. How can I help my children live their lives to the fullest?
- What is the most significant step I need to take to be a better parent? How will I know that I have succeeded?

The Octopus Parent

> **Quotable Quote:**
>
> If you stay true to your principles, you have confidence, conviction, purpose, values—in other words, you have a future.
>
> —Mike Klepper

In Nature: A group of octopuses is called a squad. There is actually no widely accepted collective noun because they don't tend to hang around in groups.

According to one group of scientists who monitored an octopus in the wild for fifty-three straight months (from a remote-controlled submarine), an octopus is a highly dedicated parent that is very much in touch with every movement of its young. This particular creature stayed with its nest for four and a half years, eating only what came around it for food. That is incredible dedication and awareness of the significance present in the parental role.

As a parent, your *Octopus* STYLE stands out because:

You are keenly aware of all of your family members and have deep convictions that guide how you lead them. You live a steadfast example for your kids. You operate your home with great intention and exemplify simplicity and strength. Though social gatherings are important, they are not your top priority.

Words you might connect with:

Attentive, adjusted, aware, equipped, and intentional.

A snapshot of the household influenced by the *Octopus* parent:

Your kids have seen you stand up for your beliefs, and they know how important your convictions are.

As a parenting partner:

You need an equally committed partner. You have a lot going on, and you will need a partner to contribute on a high level. Both of you may be Octopus parents, and you may be very loving together in your home. High boundary-setting skills are needed in your partner.

Others will know they have spotted the *Octopus* parenting STYLE when:

Octopus parents have kids living better lives than their own, and they may go to great lengths to make that happen. For many of them, a strong belief in God (or gods) is above all else. An outward expression of faith may appear to be present, but regardless, the inner heart is filled with notable commitment, dedication, and distinction.

Pros and cons of the *Octopus* parenting STYLE:

Pros: Your kids may attend private school or may be homeschooled, and they may be limited to hanging out or playing with selected friends. You may hold a restricted calendar of activities. You may give your kids decision-making opportunities through coaching or strong guidelines.

Cons: Your kids may be over-protected and might need extra care when dealing with peer pressure. They may rebel by leaving their roots behind in adult decision-making. They may not operate well outside of controlled environments. They don't have a lot of autonomy or practice with decision-making experiences.

Scriptures based on the assessment results:

"Children, do what your parents tell you. This is only right" (Ephesians 6:1).

"Don't fret or worry. Instead of worrying, pray. Let petitions and praises shape your worries into prayers, letting God know your concerns" (Philippians 4:6).

"Discipline your children while you still have the chance; indulging them destroys them" (Proverbs 19:18).

Introspective thinking:

Use this section to consider the questions and thoughts that you connect with. How can you become a better parent by considering what should be done differently? How should you actively celebrate your current successes? How should you strategize ways to connect with your children and family more intentionally?

- My kids have been taught to lean on their convictions. How do I show them what discernment looks like?
- Our family heritage is essential. How do I effectively pass that on to my children's generation so they understand the meaning of family?
- I am proud of our family and appreciate the compliments of others. How do I reflect on the things we have done well?
- Is our house peace-filled, calm, and quiet? Does everyone in our home work hard? In what ways am I teaching my kids to care for others outside of our home?

- I value the parenting experience for the long haul. As a parent, I must be patient, steady, and loyal. Where can I find encouragement in this journey?
- The future is filled with so many variables for my kids. How can I be most intentional to help guide them to hit the bullseye and not just land somewhere on the target?
- Quality over quantity is my motto. In my parenting, I desire more quality time. What is standing in the way?
- I realize my kids need time to grow up, and limiting technology helps their brains develop stronger. How can I teach my kids to be responsible for their own technology and life decisions?
- What are some ways that I can tell my kids they are on the right track?
- What is the most significant step I need to take to be a better parent? How will I know that I have succeeded?

The Ostrich Parent

> **Quotable Quote:**
>
> Being a good parent requires knowing when to push and when to back off, when to help and when to let them make mistakes, and then being strong enough to watch them go.
>
> —B. Agency

In Nature: A group of ostriches is called a flock.

Ostriches lay the largest eggs of any bird, but they often share nests with other ostrich mothers. They don't spend much time preparing their nests, which are simply divots in the ground. Ostrich parents don't actually bury their heads in the sand, though they put their heads to the ground to turn their eggs several times a day. They can run about 30 miles per hour—usually not in a straight line—but they can't fly. They are highly protective of their chicks, even when they only sense danger. Ostrich parents can be deadly and are willing to fight hard for their young.

As a parent, your *Ostrich* STYLE stands out because:

You have a lot going on, and you make things happen for your kids. They are often allowed to influence big decisions and how you spend your time. When your kids are happy, you are happy. You listen to their requests and work to meet their needs. The expectations of your kids are important to you, and you know they will thrive when you remove big obstacles from their lives. You ensure that basic necessities and your kids' needs will always be met. Your kids are your top priority—always.

Words you might connect with:

Protective, independent, selective, decisive, and sacrificial.

The Ostrich Parent

A snapshot of the household influenced by the *Ostrich* parent:

Your kids operate well in chaos and don't struggle with the constant changes you have exposed them to. It's not crazy; you see the pattern in it.

As a parenting partner:

As an Ostrich parent, you need a partner who is willing to be on the go. You need to find balance in family decision making and be willing to contribute collaboratively. Your kids might be consulted or asked for their input, but you and your partner need to make a habit of decision making, not child pleasing.

Others will know they have spotted the *Ostrich* parenting STYLE when:

You see kids who are essential family members. Ostrich parents typically consult the kids when making a family decision. More than one meal option may be served so kids can enjoy what they eat. Ostrich parents may be asked to create an excuse when kids don't want to complete homework or participate in previous commitments, *and they agree*. Ostrich parents are listeners and helpers.

Pros and cons of the *Ostrich* parenting STYLE:

Pros: Your kids have experience in decision making because they've been trained in it most of their lives. You and your kids are natural negotiators, and you all know how to express opinions. You are a master at multi-tasking. Your kids can go with the flow and adapt to frequent change.

Cons: In your home, your childrn can inadvertently possess more power than their parents- which may mean they are unsure of how to behave appropriately within other authority structures. Ostrich kids can be bossy with their peers, even if this isn't allowed at home. Ostrich kids may not understand the value of commitment or sway toward over-commitment. Priorities may dictate relational needs. Ostrich parents may find themselves working harder than others to please their kids.

Scriptures based on the assessment results:

"Post this at all the intersections, dear friends: Lead with your ears, follow up with your tongue, and let anger straggle along in the rear" (James 1:19).

"Lady Wisdom builds a lovely home; Sir Fool comes along and tears it down brick by brick" (Proverbs 14:1).

Introspective thinking:

Use this section to consider the questions and thoughts that you connect with. How can you become a

better parent by considering what should be done differently? How should you actively celebrate your current successes? How should you strategize ways to connect with your children and family more intentionally?

- Do I need to help my kids learn boundaries when talking to me? Do they need to ask my permission more often?
- As Ostrich families often do, we love to be at home. How can I help my kids learn to do their part in helping around the house?
- How can I be more realistic in my expectations of myself and my family?
- My kids may be overly sensitive or overly emotional. How can I help them find balance in those moments?
- I love that my kids know what they want. How do I help them get along with one another better? How do I help them appropriately address others who don't agree with them?
- I find it important to please my kids. How can I help them to be considerate of my needs?
- We live outside certain social norms, and I'm okay with that. Is it okay for my kids to appear different from others?
- My kids are fantastic, and I know it. Do I need to help them rein in their egos?
- Am I unaware of my children's shortcomings? Have I prepared them for adult life? What weaknesses should I be addressing now?

- What is the most significant step I need to take to be a better parent? How will I know that I have succeeded?

The Otter Parent

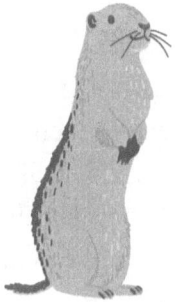

Quotable Quote:

Behind every young child who believes in himself is a parent who believed first.

—Matthew Jacobson

In Nature: A group of otters is called a raft.

Otter pups live at home until a new set is born. Otter mothers teach their pups how to hold hands with family members. Otter parents teach the pups to work together, and the drifting family group is called a raft. This is done to stay afloat. Otters do everything together as a family. They have fun and can be seen splashing and making a big to-do about nothing. Otters have been known to smile for the camera.

As a parent, your *Otter* STYLE stands out because:

You love being cool and trendy as a family unit. Your "cool" may be different from the way others define it. This unity builds positivity. You create environments and situations in which your kids will learn. You live for the perfect experience with your family and celebrate significant accomplishments. Unlike many of your friends, you want your kids to be around, and you admire them for their strengths.

Words you might connect with:

Together, positive, influential, supportive, and present.

A snapshot of the household influenced by the *Otter* parent:

Your kids know what they are good at because you tell them. You help them to be well liked.

As a parenting partner:

You need to ensure your children are not viewed as your partners. Your children need a big village, and the villagers need to understand their roles. You need a partner who appreciates and understands your creative living and parenting experiences.

The Otter Parent

Others will know they have spotted the *Otter* parenting STYLE when:

An Otter parent is known to say, "I am a giver, I'm cool, and I want my kid to like me above all else," or "I want my kid to grow up to be my best friend, and I don't mind if that happens before he grows up." The Otter parent may also say to the kids, "We don't care if you do taboo, harmful, or experimental things; just do them at home." Otter parents want their friends to like their kids and assume they do.

Pros and cons of the *Otter* parenting STYLE:

Pros: You feel you have an open relationship with your kids where you share and communicate back and forth. Your kids love that you choose to be present. Your children's friends like them. You and your kids are well liked on social media.

Cons: Your kids may not recognize the relationship between actions and their consequences. They may need more boundaries, or they may struggle with authority outside of your influence. You may feel pressured to spend excessive money on your kids to impress friends. Your kids may have trouble understanding that not all adults are their friends, especially their teachers or bosses.

Scriptures based on the assessment results:

"Wise discipline imparts wisdom; spoiled adolescents embarrass their parents" (Proverbs 29:15).

"Be even-tempered, content with second place, quick to forgive an offense. Forgive as quickly and completely as the Master forgave you" (Colossians 3:13).

"A good life gets passed on to the grandchildren; ill-gotten wealth ends up with good people" (Proverbs 13:22).

Introspective thinking:

Use this section to consider the questions and thoughts that you connect with. How can you become a better parent by considering what should be done differently? How should you actively celebrate your current successes? How should you strategize ways to connect with your children and family more intentionally?

- I need my children around; do they need me, too?
- Do my children like me as much as I want them to?
- My children know I love them, but not everyone does. Have I helped them learn how to make friends with others who might not easily like them?

- My kids are special and often successful. Have I prepared them for both winning and losing in life?
- I should have budgeted for this, but oh well, you only live once, right? How can I teach my child about finances and priorities in a healthy way?
- My kids know how much I appreciate them—I think! How do I ensure that they know?
- I like my kids more than I like yours. Am I too judgmental when it comes to the flaws in my children's friends?
- I've heard that mentors are great for growth. How can I help my children find additional influences in their lives?
- How am I encouraging my children to make friends with people their own age?
- What is the most significant step I need to take to be a better parent? How will I know that I have succeeded?

The Owl Parent

> **Quotable Quote:**
>
> The mediocre teacher tells, the good teacher explains,
> the superior teacher demonstrates,
> and the great teacher inspires.
>
> —William A. Ward

In Nature: A group of owls is called a parliament.

When we think of an owl's persona, we automatically think of intelligence or wisdom. Throughout history, the owl has been used as a symbol of wisdom. This has been represented in stories from the Iliad, Winnie the Pooh, and even Merlin, who was often described as an owl. In ancient Greece, the owl was used as a symbol for the Greek goddess Athena. In many cultures, owls represent knowledge and wisdom because of their watchfulness at night. Whether owls are actually wise is debated, but the symbolism is strong.

As a parent, your *Owl* STYLE stands out because:

You know that life is hard and that setting your kids up for success is critical. Adulthood hinges on three key elements that your kids must adopt: a good job, a well-prepared portfolio, and the education needed to make it all happen. The knowledge your children gain will come from every aspect of their lives, and teaching them to discover the importance of each opportunity will help them learn to manage their own lives more successfully. Every day is a chance to learn something new. Discernment and understanding help your kids sort out bad examples from good ones. Kids grow from knowledge, implementation, and application.

Words you might connect with:

Counsel, expectations, education, guidance, and wisdom.

A snapshot of the household influenced by the *Owl* parent:

Your kids know the importance of education and the need to obtain skills to be what they want to be as adults.

As a parenting partner:

As an Owl, you value good grades, hard work, and problem-solving, and you need a partner who does the same. Wisdom and knowledge come from understanding, experiencing, and education, and you will need a partner in every aspect of your parenting to help round out your children's expectations. Balance and stability are key roles in your partnership, as is collaborative conversation.

Others will know they have spotted the *Owl* parenting STYLE when:

Owls prepare quietly and know how to make well-calculated moves. This has helped them to be seen as wise and precise. Owls appear to be knowledgeable and to have great perception. They study before they hunt and get what they are most focused on.

Pros and cons of the *Owl* parenting STYLE:

Pros: Your children know the value of good grades. They work hard to please you. They grasp the value of true wisdom, and they know the difference between wisdom and knowledge.

Cons: Sometimes, too much focus on grades can make the your children feel that they can't earn your approval. Your kids may be good students but not good at executing what they've learned or to understand that application matters. They may need to be taught common sense or gentleness, and not just to learn facts.

Scriptures based on the assessment results:

"Write these commandments that I've given you today on your hearts. Get them inside of you and then get them inside your children. Talk about them wherever you are, sitting at home or walking in the street; talk about them from the time you get up in the morning to when you fall into bed at night" (Deuteronomy 6:6–7).

"I'm speaking to you out of deep gratitude for all that God has given me, and especially as I have responsibilities in relation to you. Living then, as every one of you does, in pure grace, it's important that you not misinterpret yourselves as people who are bringing this goodness to God. No, God brings it all to you. The only accurate way to understand ourselves is by what God is and by what he does for us, not by what we are and what we do for him" (Romans 12:3).

"If you don't know what you're doing, pray to the Father. He loves to help. You'll get his help, and won't be condescended to when you ask for it. Ask boldly, believingly, without a second thought. People who 'worry their prayers' are like wind-whipped waves" (James 1:5–6).

Introspective thinking:

Use this section to consider the questions and thoughts that you connect with. How can you become a better parent by considering what should be done differently? How should you actively celebrate your current

successes? How should you strategize ways to connect with your children and family more intentionally?

- I have been heard saying, "Go do your homework; you're going to need those skills in life." What other skills do my kids need?
- Where should we hang their diploma(s)? And what other memories do we need to make?
- Being the best means I have put in the hard work, and there will be a time to show what I have accomplished. How do I help my kids always give their best?
- Goals, benchmarks, and grades are the measurement of success in education. How can I help my kids find satisfaction in other areas of life?
- Am I keenly aware of moments when my kids manipulate others? Do they act out through rule-breaking or defiance? How can I address them?
- How can I help my children value their peers? What about when my kids don't achieve well in school? Do I know how to respond when they fail? Do they?
- Interpersonal skills are important for all kids to learn. How am I helping my children learn these skills?
- Jim Trelease said, "A child spends 7,800 hours at home and 900 hours in class during one school year." Which teacher should be most accountable?
- How would I grade myself on providing teachable moments for my kids?

- What is the most significant step I need to take to be a better parent? How will I know that I have succeeded?

The Penguin Parent

> **Quotable Quote:**
>
> Too much love never spoils children.
> Children become spoiled when we substitute presents for presence.
>
> —Anthony Whitman

In Nature: A group of penguins is called a waddle.

The penguin is an excellent example of an animal that loves to give magnificent gifts—if you like rocks. The male penguin will search for the perfect rock to give his hopeful love as part of their courtship. She accepts the rock only if she plans to return her affection. Penguins use rocks to build their future nests. The male has even been known to steal a rock from another nest to present as a gift.

As a parent, your *Penguin* STYLE stands out because:

You are a gift-giver extraordinaire. You know when to surprise someone with something special. You know where to get great sales. That's not as important as the look on your child's face when you have surpassed expectations. Everyone else has holidays, but you know how to make any day of the week special. You don't like to be obligated to offer a reward, and you teach your children to find excitement in anything given to them—small, medium, or large. You are willing to sacrifice for the right moment, and you are eager to help your children find happiness, even in the hard times.

Words you might connect with:

Generosity, happiness, joy, spontaneous, and value.

A snapshot of the household influenced by the *Penguin* parent:

Your kids know how to say "thank you." They have a large vocabulary to explain their level of satisfaction, and they see the power of a moment.

The Penguin Parent

As a parenting partner:

As a Penguin, you are a joyful giver, and you need a partner who wants to receive gifts or who joins in giving to the kids. Someone with a sacrificial parenting style will pair well with you, but both of you must be cautious to keep the home in balance. Your partner must understand the role of gifts within the family budget.

Others will know they have spotted the *Penguin* parenting STYLE when:

Love and generosity are a considerable part of the Penguin family unit. Penguin parents find great satisfaction in wooing their children and friends, and they love the moment a gift is revealed. Penguin parents may be shoppers, but more importantly, they are givers, and not every gift is purchased.

Pros and cons of the *Penguin* parenting STYLE:

Pros: You show your kids great affection, and they have experienced it often. They know they are loved. Encouraging words are often shared as gifts among members of your family. Your childen grow up with good taste in material possessions and relationships.

Cons: Your kids may expect or even demand gifts at inappropriate times. They may learn to be picky as gift recipients, and they may be ungrateful if gifts are not good enough. Finances may limit the ability to give gifts in your home. Misdirected gift-givers may have difficulty expressing themselves or may unintentionally manipulate others through gifts.

Scriptures based on the assessment results:

"We can boldly quote, 'God is there, ready to help; I'm fearless no matter what. Who or what can get to me?'" (Hebrews 13:6).

"Speaking to the people, he went on, 'Take care! Protect yourself against the least bit of greed. Life is not defined by what you have, even when you have a lot'" (Luke 12:15).

"Don't hoard treasure down here where it gets eaten by moths and corroded by rust or—worse!—stolen by burglars. Stockpile treasure in heaven, where it's safe from moth and rust and burglars. It's obvious, isn't it? The place where your treasure is, is the place you will most want to be, and end up being" (Matthew 6:19–21).

Introspective thinking

Use this section to consider the questions and thoughts that you connect with. How can you become a better parent by considering what should be done differently? How should you actively celebrate your current successes? How should you strategize ways to connect with your children and family more intentionally?

- Small, expensive, and big gifts are how I show my children that I'm paying attention. How else can I show them affection?
- I may not be as invested as you think, and you may think I'm not affectionate, but I care deeply. Sometimes others see my gift-giving as bribery. How do I ensure that people see my motives in the right light?
- Love and life don't operate at the same speed. How can I find balance and peace in my parenting?
- It's not that my kids are ungrateful (most of the time), but sometimes I notice that they don't show appreciation. How can I help them express their gratitude, especially toward others?
- I am often compelled to give my child something meaningful to remember a moment. How else can we make memories?
- How do I react when my children are demanding or manipulative? What healthy tools do I need to develop in my parenting toolbox?
- Generosity comes from my most inner core. What steps do I need to take to help my kids learn to be generous, too?
- What limitations do I see in my parenting style? Why? How do they steal my joy?
- Describe the most meaningful gift or experience you could ever have with your child. What would make the moment top the charts?

- What is the most significant step I need to take to be a better parent? How will I know that I have succeeded?

The Possum Parent

> **Quotable Quote:**
>
> My parents are my backbone. Still are.
> They are the only group that will support you
> if you score zero or if you score 40.
>
> —Kobe Bryant

In Nature: A group of possums is called a passel.

Possums are known to be very peaceful animals that carry their young on their back. They prefer to avoid fights or conflicts at all cost. This creature has an involuntary mechanism to play dead. The stress of confrontation causes the possum to go into shock or a comatose state. This can last anywhere from forty minutes to an hour. While this ability can save the possum from its predators, it is not helpful when it happens in the middle of the road.

As a parent, your *Possum* STYLE stands out because:

You love how much you can brag about your kids. They are great! They are independent and strong. No matter what, you will always be proud of them, and you are careful not to pry into their personal lives as they grow older. You see potential, and you know your kids will find their way. Your optimism carries you through those moments when you carry your kids and their struggles.

Words you might connect with:

Peaceful, optimistic, determined, resourceful, and strong.

A snapshot of the household influenced by the *Possum* parent:

You may have one or ten, but your kids know you are not there to micromanage their world. You see the big picture, and you know your kids can stay clear of conflict and danger.

As a parenting partner:

As a Possum parent, you may be a little cynical and often overly realistic. You may visualize the worst in decision-making. Your partner needs to bring positivity and strength. You need a solid decision-maker to help run the home. You need rest and downtime, and your partner needs to understand this important part of your pace.

Others will know they have spotted the *Possum* parenting STYLE when:

The Possum parent can see the flaws in most situations and navigate around them. When a moment of indecision is reached, the Possum parent may struggle but will always try to support the kids.

Pros and cons of the *Possum* parenting STYLE:

Pros: Your kids feel supported by you, and they know you believe in them. There is a lot of optimism in your home mixed with idealized expectations. Your children's best interest is seen by you above all others.

Cons: Your kids may easily fool you. They have a tendency to be deceitful while pacifying your expectations. You may defend this behavior in your kids, and you may ignore warning signs of bad choices they are making.

Scriptures based on the assessment results:

"Point your kids in the right direction—when they're old they won't be lost" (Proverbs 22:6).

"A good life gets passed on to the grandchildren; ill-gotten wealth ends up with good people" (Proverbs 13:22).

"At the time, discipline isn't much fun. It always feels like it's going against the grain. Later, of course, it pays off big-time, for it's the well-trained who find themselves mature in their relationship with God" (Hebrews 12:11).

Introspective thinking:

Use this section to consider the questions and thoughts that you connect with. How can you become a better parent by considering what should be done differently? How should you actively celebrate your current successes? How should you strategize ways to connect with your children and family more intentionally?

- As a Possum parent, I am not easily shaken. What fears do I have when it comes to parenting?
- Worldview changes who a person is. How do I work to shape my children's worldview?
- It is vital to separate love and punishment. How have I done this well?
- How does my child's stubbornness create struggle in my day?
- What systems have I put into place to make my family function efficiently? Are they working?
- How will I respond if my child gives me disappointing news? How can I be prepared for unexpected moments before they arrive?
- What stands in the way of my wise decision making? What do I need to do to lead my children successfully?

The Possum Parent

- Am I procrastinating on making choices or even avoiding them when it comes to my children?
- Who is my support system as I parent this family?
- What is the most significant step I need to take to be a better parent? How will I know that I have succeeded?

The Raccoon Parent

> **Quotable Quote:**
>
> Parents can only give good advice or put them on the right path. But the final forming of a person's character lies in their own hands.
>
> —Anne Frank

In Nature: A group of raccoons is called a nursery.

The raccoon has the scientific name *Procyon lotor*, literally meaning "washing bear." It has been noted that raccoons will not wash plants as much as they do meat. This shows they know the difference, but it also suggests that they think meat is dirtier. Even if water isn't available, the raccoon will look as if it is wiping off its food. Some scientists don't actually believe raccoons are rinsing their food as much as playing in the water. One interesting fact is that they are careful not to remove earthworms or insects when they wash—extra protein, you know.

As a parent, your *Raccoon* STYLE stands out because:

You are not like everyone else. You stand up for what you know to be correct. That might make you seem different from others, but you know what is suitable for your family. You are not driven to be a conformist. You are choosy and research savvy. There are dozens of answers for every opportunity you encounter, and you are good at finding the top options. Your work on the front end provides excellent results on the back end. You hope your kids will grow up to be the best because you have paved the way for success.

Words you might connect with:

Selective, community, aware, intentional, and quality.

A snapshot of the household influenced by the *Raccoon* parent:

Your kids are laid back about things that might excite others. They live with different standards, and it's okay if outsiders can't see or understand them.

The Raccoon Parent

As a parenting partner:

Your unconventional ideas might not work for everyone. Your partner must appreciate and support your unique outlook on life. Nature over nurture is the key to this partnership. You enjoy quality experiences, and your partner needs to understand what that quality is.

Others will know they have spotted the *Raccoon* parenting STYLE when:

A Raccoon parent can be identified by the use of cloth diapers, essential oils, yoga, or even a healthy appreciation for hemp products. These have a place in the world, along with alternative therapies or educational choices.

Pros and cons of the *Raccoon* parenting STYLE:

Pros: Your kids are laid back in their expectations. They are healthy because you make this a priority. Your children learn in the home and in natural settings. They have an innate appreciation for nature and wild things.

Cons: Your kids may have trouble showing respect toward those with conventional values. They may not fit in well with their peers. They may be overly optimistic, take advantage of others, be taken advantage of, or assume an entirely pessimistic role. Your children may be teased due to the unconventional lifestyle of your family.

Scriptures based on the assessment results:

"Get along with each other; don't be stuck-up. Make friends with nobodies; don't be the great somebody" (Romans 12:16).

"Don't you see that children are God's best gift? the fruit of the womb his generous legacy?" (Psalm 127:3).

"If your child asks for bread, do you trick him with sawdust? If he asks for fish, do you scare him with a live snake on his plate?" (Matthew 7:9–10).

Introspective thinking:

Use this section to consider the questions and thoughts which you connect with. How can you become a better parent by simply considering what should be done differently? How should you actively celebrate your current successes? How should you strategize ways to connect with your children and family more intentionally?

- My kids need to be healthy. Their hearts, minds, and souls matter. How am I intentional about these choices?
- My kids are not one-dimensional. How am I teaching them to be mature and well-rounded?
- I encourage strong independence and individuality with my kids. How am I letting them be themselves while respecting others in the process?

- My kids can solve problems because social constraints don't box them in. Do I allow them to struggle in the problem-solving phase? How else can I help them grow?
- I emphasize tradition over convention when it comes to health and safety in our home. How far will I reach to find new habits and conventions for our family?
- Do I have a keen eye for finding the best of everything? How will I develop my kids to become world changers?
- There are best practices for parenting in every culture. How does my worldview affect which practices I put in place? Is my filter strong enough?
- How is my influence affecting our family unity? How can I improve our relationships?
- How can I be more adaptable? How can I learn to pivot and be willing to try new things?
- What is the most significant step I need to take to be a better parent? How will I know that I have succeeded?

The Turtle Parent

> **Quotable Quote:**
>
> A concerted effort to preserve our heritage
> is a vital link to our cultural, educational,
> and economic legacies—all of the things that quite
> literally make us who we are.
>
> —Steve Berry

In Nature: A group of turtles is called a bale.

The sea turtle is remarkable in how she will lay her eggs in the same place where she was hatched herself. Scientists believe that turtles view this as "It was good enough for me, so it's good enough for my young." Scientists have many theories about how a sea turtle is able to find its place of origin. The fact that it can go thousands of miles away and still return is quite remarkable! Turtles have deep habits that span generations and are passed on by parents to their young.

As a parent, your *Turtle* STYLE stands out because:

You are intelligent, wise, and want your kids to succeed—no matter what. You have very high expectations, and you believe they can be met. You have great respect for the past, and you honor your rich family history. You are a storyteller, and it is essential for your kids to carry on your family's legacy. Your home may display heirlooms that your children are taught to respect. Your kids must grow up to honor your family name and traditions.

Words you might connect with:

Respect, loyal, legacy, connectedness, and thoughtful.

A snapshot of the household influenced by the *Turtle* parent:

Your children are given great opportunities to learn and improve. Your entire family knows that you have priorities that must be appreciated. Your kids will grow up with natural time management and precision skills that are unique to your parenting STYLE.

As a parenting partner:

Keeping expectations and future planning at the forefront is vital for this partnership. As a Turtle, you need help teaching your kids to collect heirlooms, not just stuff. You need to be encouraged, and you need a partner who is willing to stick with you for the long haul. This partnership must have maturity and mutual respect to last.

Others will know they have spotted the *Turtle* parenting STYLE when:

Inside the home of the Turtle parent, you will find collected items of value. The parents may not flaunt it, but they will think their kid is smarter than yours. Turtle parents have been known to buy flashcards and pay for professional tutoring, so their children's grades will be higher than anyone else's. Their crowning achievement will happen when their children are thriving as adults. Time management is a family trade secret.

Pros and cons of the *Turtle* parenting STYLE:

Pros: Your kids are used to hard work and perseverance. They can spot a typo with no difficulty. They are well-read and are typically seen as good students. Your children know the importance of education. They tend to graduate with higher degrees from college; therefore, they may have higher-paying jobs and they will often manage businesses or lead teams.

Cons: Your children may struggle with how to deal with failure. Small failures or big mistakes may feel similar. Most of the time, their drive comes from you and often not their own self-motivation. Your kids might thrive in trying to outsmart authority or peers. They might not know how to survive on their own without their parents.

Scriptures based on the assessment results:

"Be good friends who love deeply; practice playing second fiddle" (Romans 12:10).

"Start with God—the first step in learning is bowing down to God; only fools thumb their noses at such wisdom and learning" (Proverbs 1:7).

"You're one happy man when you do what's right, one happy woman when you form the habit of justice" (Psalm 106:3).

Introspective thinking:

Use this section to consider the questions and thoughts that you connect with. How can you become a better parent by considering what should be done differently? How should you actively celebrate your current successes? How should you strategize ways to connect with your children and family more intentionally?

- I'm proud of my kids, though that doesn't always mean they are doing well. How can I support each of my kids today, even in their struggles?
- I don't always like what my kids do, but I love them deeply. In what new ways could I show

- this? How do I show unconditional love, even in disappointing moments?
- Legacy runs deep in our family. I want my kids to keep this tradition going. What are some ideas for encouraging them to share in this passion?
- Do I encourage my kids to be humble, kind, and compassionate? How do I see them living out these values?
- "Do as I do" is a mantra in our home. Am I modeling foundational skills for my kids to see?
- My kids have struggled, but they know True North. Am I prepared for moments when they lose their way or choose not to follow my lead? How am I helping them to trust their gut instinct from a young age and to make good decisions?
- Context is everything. Helping my children understand the meaning and value of words and appropriate actions falls in the context of our family's story. In what ways do I help my kids see the cause and effect of their actions?
- You always want your kids to get it right. Consider this: Am I helping my kids find value, even when they don't get it right?
- I can't control others, but I want my kids to live their best lives. Have I set them up well? How do I truly feel?
- What is the most significant step I need to take to be a better parent? How will I know that I have succeeded?

The Whale Parent

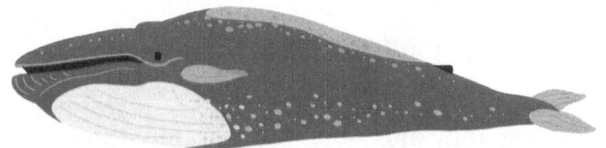

> **Quotable Quote:**
>
> Respond to your children with love in their
> worst moments, their broken moments,
> their angry moments, their selfish moments,
> their lonely moments, their frustrating moments,
> their inconvenient moments, because it is in their
> most unlovable human moments that
> they most need to feel loved.
>
> —L.R. Knost

In Nature: A group of whales is called a pod.

There is a debate about whether the blue whale or the sperm whale is the loudest animal in the sea. Nevertheless, the whale as a species is one of the loudest animals on earth, sounding at 188 decibels. Compare this to fireworks exploding in the sky or the sound of a flying jet plane. Amazingly, 194 decibels are the loudest a human can hear. This makes the whale a very loud animal. A whale parent's call can top them all when necessary.

As a parent, your *Whale* STYLE stands out because:

You are fun, and you look for fun things to do. You look into the future, get excited with possibilities, and help your kids know that bigger and better things are ahead. Others know when you are coming because your family is loud and you are right in the middle of the action. You are in charge of your kids, and your command lets everyone know you mean business. The level of activity in your home is very high, and your kids know exactly what they want.

Words you might connect with:

Active, improving, ambitious, energetic, and honest.

A snapshot of the household influenced by the *Whale* parent:

Your kids have been taught to dream, to think forward, and to respond to you quickly. When you speak, your kids know your voice, even in a crowded room.

As a parenting partner:

You need a partner who can balance your bold parenting voice and the commanding presence you have with your children. Activity and chaos can be managed with the right partnership if you're on the same wavelength. You need someone who understands your stress points and is able to help diffuse a situation when you are frustrated.

Others will know they have spotted the *Whale* parenting STYLE when:

A Whale parent gets excited about what is ahead and wants the whole family to know about it. This parent may be the loudest person in the room, but that's okay, because fun is the most important thing. The Whale wants everybody to cooperate, but when nobody listens, this parent just get louder than the noise.

Pros and cons of the *Whale* parenting STYLE:

Pros: Your kids know the role of authority in the food chain. They know your expectations, hopefully ahead of time. Your children find your home to be a great place to hang out. You want your home to be efficient and for everyone to cooperate, and you love it when everything comes together.

Cons: Your kids tend to tune you out if there is too much yelling or chaos. They may comply simply to appease you. Your children may avoid being home in their teen and young adult years. They may become argumentative and even rude to you, their peers, or anyone they feel is demanding of them. They may feel your expectations are too demanding and that their voices cannot be heard by others.

Scriptures based on the assessment results:

"Fathers, don't frustrate your children with no-win scenarios. Take them by the hand and lead them in the way of the Master" (Ephesians 6:4).

"Friends, don't complain about each other. A far greater complaint could be lodged against you, you know. The Judge is standing just around the corner" (James 5:9).

"Sing hymns instead of drinking songs! Sing songs from your heart to Christ" (Ephesians 5:19).

Introspective thinking:

Use this section to consider the questions and thoughts that you connect with. How can you become a better parent by considering what should be done differently? How should you actively celebrate your current successes? How should you strategize ways to connect with your children and family more intentionally?

- My opinions matter, and I don't have any trouble expressing what they are. How can I communicate them gently with my kids?
- How am I helping others to help my kids? (Think teachers, coaches, leaders, grandparents, etc.)

- My kids know how to act; I just wish they would. I hate it when others criticize them. What must I do to accept this better?
- I know the right way to do things, and I can tell you how. That doesn't mean I know how to parent. What parenting advice do I need today?
- Efficiency is my downfall, but I have a lot of initiative to make up for that. In what one area of our home would it be most helpful to add a step toward efficiency right now?
- I would love to have peace and harmony at home, and it does show up every once in a while. How do my expectations promote this end goal? Am I communicating that goal effectively?
- Chaos is not a problem; I can operate in that arena well. What stress does that cause for my family and friends when chaos is present so often?
- My influence is meaningful. Do I self-reflect and make adjustments, or do I just keep doing things the same way repeatedly, even when they don't work?
- Most kids learn that the path of least resistance is the best one to take. Am I setting my kids up to win in the world, or just to avoid things that challenge them?
- What is the most significant step I need to take to be a better parent? How will I know that I have succeeded?

www.ingramcontent.com/pod-product-compliance
Lightning Source LLC
Chambersburg PA
CBHW020228170426
43201CB00007B/353